Guest-edited by Marcus White and Jane Burry

LOFTY IDEALS TO SHOCKING REALITIES

AD

01 | Vol 93 | 2023

URBAN DYSTOPIAS   01/2023

About the Guest-Editors   5

Marcus White and Jane Burry

Introduction   6

A Truly Golden Handbook of Urban DYStopias

Marcus White and Jane Burry

Urban Farming   14

The Reluctant Utopia

Daniele Belleri and Carlo Ratti

Pertopia   22

Speculative Thinking in a Short-Term World

Justyna Karakiewicz

Broadband-acre City   30

'No Traffic Problem, No Buffering'

Marcus White and Stephen Glackin

The Mega-Eco-Garden City   38

Stories of Rewilding and Ecodystopia

Nano Langenheim and Kongjian Yu

An Urban Odyssey   46

City Beautiful to City Instagrammable

Jordi Oliveras

Arcological City   54

Going Underground

Jane Burry and Mehrnoush Latifi

Cool Urbanism   62

The Radiant Exitance City

Marcus White and Tianyi Yang

The City of Frictionless Mobility   72

Ian Woodcock

ISSN 0003-8504 ISBN 9781 119 833994

Edited by **Marcus White and Jane Burry**

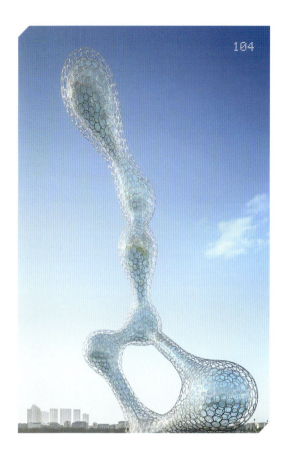

High-Definition City 80
An Invisible Horizon of Technological Human Space

Andong Lu, Jane Burry and Marcus White

The Promises of Postcolonial Utopias 88
Perspectives from the Global South

Tridib Banerjee

Cité Industrielle 4.0 96
Zoning for the Latest Revolution

Jane Burry

Another Normal 104
A Techno-Social Alternative to Techno-Feudal Cities

Kas Oosterhuis

The Floating 'Urban Village' 112
Makoko Futures

Dan Nyandega

GAN-Physarum 120
Shaping the Future of the Urbansphere

Claudia Pasquero and Marco Poletto

This issue of △ explores the dichotomy between idealised visions for the design of urban settlements and the potentially shocking realities which may emerge from those same impulses and intentions

— Marcus White and Jane Burry

From Another Perspective 128

Fanning the Flames of the City Heat

Anton Markus Pasing

Neil Spiller

Contributors 134

Editorial Offices
John Wiley & Sons
9600 Garsington Road
Oxford
OX4 2DQ

T +44 (0)18 6577 6868

Editor
Neil Spiller

Managing Editor
Caroline Ellerby
Caroline Ellerby Publishing

Freelance Contributing Editor
Abigail Grater

Publisher
Todd Green

Art Direction + Design
Christian Küsters
Mihaela Mincheva
CHK Design

Production Editor
Elizabeth Gongde

Prepress
Artmedia, London

Printed in the United Kingdom by Hobbs the Printers Ltd

Front cover
Harrison and White with Flood Slicer, Implementing the Rhetoric, Footscray, Victoria, Australia, 2010. © Harrison and White with Flood Slicer.

Inside front cover
Shi Percy Pan, Yingna Celina Sun and Jiaao Wayne Wong, The Great Ocean Road is Crying in Tears of Plastic, Studio 05, Melbourne School of Design, University of Melbourne, Australia, 2021. Shi Percy Pan, Yingna Celina Sun and Jiaao Wayne Wong

Page 1
Kundi Shu, Kachung Lo and Xiufeng Li, Rhizomatic bridge as a hope in Peturbanism: Aquaculture and Aquatics scenario, Hope in Peturbanism – Possible Future of Great Ocean [Road?] CDE Studio 05, Melbourne School of Design, University of Melbourne, Australia, 2021. © Kundi Shu, Kachung Lo and Xiufeng Li

EDITORIAL BOARD

Denise Bratton
Paul Brislin
Mark Burry
Helen Castle
Nigel Coates
Peter Cook
Kate Goodwin
Edwin Heathcote
Brian McGrath
Jayne Merkel
Peter Murray
Mark Robbins
Deborah Saunt
Patrik Schumacher
Jill Stoner
Ken Yeang

ARCHITECTURAL DESIGN
January/February 2023
Issue 01
Profile No. 278

Disclaimer
The Publisher and Editors cannot be held responsible for errors or any consequences arising from the use of information contained in this journal; the views and opinions expressed do not necessarily reflect those of the Publisher and Editors, neither does the publication of advertisements constitute any endorsement by the Publisher and Editors of the products advertised.

MIX
Paper from responsible sources
FSC® C015829

Journal Customer Services
For ordering information, claims and any enquiry concerning your journal subscription please go to www.wileycustomerhelp.com/ask or contact your nearest office.

Americas
E: cs-journals@wiley.com
T: +1 877 762 2974

Europe, Middle East and Africa
E: cs-journals@wiley.com
T: +44 (0)1865 778 315

Asia Pacific
E: cs-journals@wiley.com
T: +65 6511 8000

Japan (for Japanese-speaking support)
E: cs-japan@wiley.com
T: +65 6511 8010

Visit our Online Customer Help available in 7 languages at www.wileycustomerhelp.com/ask

Print ISSN: 0003-8504
Online ISSN: 1554-2769

Prices are for six issues and include postage and handling charges. Individual-rate subscriptions must be paid by personal cheque or credit card. Individual-rate subscriptions may not be resold or used as library copies.

All prices are subject to change without notice.

Identification Statement
Periodicals Postage paid at Rahway, NJ 07065. Air freight and mailing in the USA by Mercury Media Processing, 1850 Elizabeth Avenue, Suite C, Rahway, NJ 07065, USA.

USA Postmaster
Please send address changes to *Architectural Design*, John Wiley & Sons Inc., c/o The Sheridan Press, PO Box 465, Hanover, PA 17331, USA

Rights and Permissions
Requests to the Publisher should be addressed to:
Permissions Department
John Wiley & Sons Ltd
The Atrium
Southern Gate
Chichester
West Sussex PO19 8SQ
UK

F: +44 (0)1243 770 620
E: Permissions@wiley.com

All Rights Reserved. No part of this publication may be reproduced, stored in a retrieval system or transmitted in any form or by any means, electronic, mechanical, photocopying, recording, scanning or otherwise, except under the terms of the Copyright, Designs and Patents Act 1988 or under the terms of a licence issued by the Copyright Licensing Agency Ltd, 5th Floor, Shackleton House, Battle Bridge Lane, London SE1 2HX, without the permission in writing of the Publisher.

Subscribe to *D*
D is published bimonthly and is available to purchase on both a subscription basis and as individual volumes at the following prices.

Prices
Individual copies:
£29.99 / US$45.00
Mailing fees for print may apply

Annual Subscription Rates
Student: £97 / US$151 print only
Personal: £151 / US$236 print only
Institutional: £357 / US$666 online only
Institutional: £373 / US$695 print only
Institutional: £401 / US$748 print and online

ABOUT THE GUEST-EDITORS

MARCUS WHITE AND JANE BURRY

Longstanding academic colleagues Marcus White and Jane Burry have worked to knit together the tectonics of architecture and a deeper engagement with the urban realm, adopting accessible and applicable technologies and digital data to deepen the contextual grounding. At the Swinburne University of Technology, where White is Professor of Architecture and Urban Design, and Burry is Professor and Dean of the School of Design and Architecture, they have been instrumental in co-authoring a unique combined Master's programme in architecture and urban design. Proponents of the integration of education with research and practice, White is a partner in the award-winning architecture practice Harrison and White (HAW), while Burry's research leverages her experience as a project architect in the technical team at the Sagrada Família in Barcelona.

Both share a deep interest in speculative futures, including micro-scaled digital fabrication inquiry; investigating sonic and thermal experience at the interface of built fabric, people and air; innovation in construction methods; and macro-scaled explorations of radical urban propositions imagining new ways of living. Their work is conducted through their research within the Spatio-Temporal Research Urban Design and Architecture Laboratory (STRÜDAL) at Swinburne's Centre for Design Innovation. Their enduring commitment to the exploration of computationally enabled design futures exposes them to the endlessly divergent possibilities, some markedly dark, that artificially intelligent and algorithmic urbanisms can invoke.

White's work focuses on research for and through design, using emerging technology and data to design liveable cities. He is the creator of the pedestrian network analysis tool www.PedestrianCatch.com, and led the City of Melbourne Sunlight Public Open Space Study (2018) in developing new methodologies to protect sunlight amenity for the city. He is also a chief investigator in the Neuro-Optimised Virtual Living Lab (NOVELL) with the Florey Institute of Neuroscience and Mental Health, which recently won a European Healthcare Design Award (2022), and leads the Australian Research Council (ARC)-funded 'Walk-Quality' Linkage Project. He is co-author, with Nano Langenheim, of the book *The Death of Urbanism: Transitions Through Five Stages of Grief* (Art Architecture Design Research [AADR], 2020), a metamodern exploration of urban design paradigms through a misappropriation of Elisabeth Kübler-Ross's five stages of grief.

Burry is the lead author of *The New Mathematics of Architecture* (Thames & Hudson, 2010), editor of *Designing the Dynamic* (Melbourne Books, 2013) and co-author of *Prototyping for Architects* (Thames & Hudson, 2016), as well as over a hundred other publications. She has practised, taught, supervised and researched internationally. She is a recipient of six Australian Research Council grants, Good Design Awards and the Robots in Architecture Pioneer's Award. Her research focuses on mathematics and computing in contemporary design. Recent partnered research explores the opportunities for urban and biometric data gathering and application in modelling; simulation and application for the design of better urban environments; and leveraging digital fabrication with simulation and feedback to create better, more sensitive, human-centric spaces. By manipulating geometry and materiality within the design, architecture can fine tune the acoustic, thermal and airflow aesthetics to create higher-quality, energy-efficient environments in buildings and the urban realm. ᴆ

Text © 2023 John Wiley & Sons Ltd. Images: (t) © Marcus White; (b) © Jane Burry

INTRODUCTION

MARCUS WHITE AND JANE BURRY

A TRULY GOLDEN HANDBOOK OF URBAN DYSTOPIAS

Kundi Shu, Kachung Lo and Xiufeng Li, Rhizomatic bridge as a hope in Peturbanism: Aquaculture and Aquatics scenario, Hope in Peturbanism – Possible Future of Great Ocean [Road?] CDE Studio 05, Melbourne School of Design, University of Melbourne, Australia, 2021

Section drawing of aquaculture and aquatic activities for the exploratory design studio project exploring the integration of natural and man-made dynamic adaptive systems and the reuse of waste materials for ecological restoration. Studio leader: Justyna Karakiewicz

Cities are facing several coinciding global crises. There is the dominant existential narrative of the impacts of climate change and the need to adapt to them. Resilient architecture and urban planning are needed in response to the unprecedented urbanisation and economic growth that have impacted environments worldwide. New approaches to nature and food production, new modes of transport, renewed anxiety about robots replacing human workforces, ever-accelerating advances in information technology and the humbling recent experience of a global pandemic are challenging norms and expectations. These factors, all with the potential to foster social division, are changing life experiences of populations worldwide, giving rise to the authoritarian politics of anxiety and creating the sense that people are teetering between radically different possible futures.

This issue of ⌂ explores the dichotomy between idealised visions for the design of urban settlements and the potentially shocking realities which may emerge from those same impulses and intentions. It examines the slippery territory between utopias – the idealised places Oscar Wilde believed humankind sets sail for, and must realise, for progress to take place[1] – and some of the ensuing dystopias in urban design that unfold instead.

Each article re-explores a commonly dismissed historic urban-utopian proposition to test its relevance through the lens of a critical contemporary urban challenge. Each considers both a utopian and dystopian speculative reinterpretation of these potential urban futures, teasing out the elements leading to a desirable future as well as those pointing to unintended malign consequences.

Utopia Versus Dystopia and the Need for Speculative Futures

Predictions of the future are always speculative. The further out our forecasts reach, the more speculative and stochastic they become. Although our speculations are built upon historical data, the future is not the past and the past never repeats itself. Nevertheless, we have both an endless appetite and a serious need for speculative futures. They are the basis for planning and it is critical that in constructing and examining them we embrace both hope and scepticism. This is a story about reclaiming the urban design narrative and being alert to the potential impacts of socio-technical decision-making and design in cities.

In their influential book *Speculative Everything: Design, Fiction, And Social Dreaming* (2013),[2] Anthony Dunne and Fiona Raby of the New York design studio Dunne & Raby describe futurist Stuart Candy's concept of four kinds of design speculations: probable, plausible, possible and preferable. Here, 'probable' refers to projections of scenarios that are likely to occur; 'plausible' forecasts alternative economic and political scenarios that may occur; 'possible' is far more radical, incorporating what is scientifically and technically possible; and 'preferable' represents an intersection of probable and plausible.

While not attempting to predict the future, these speculations are suggested as a way to engage with what might be considered pathways to desirable futures. This approach has similarities with the future-casting methods of multinational energy and mining companies that model available resources, future demand, the likely impacts of lobbying and investment, and the profit gained by ensuring that legislation to mitigate climate change is delayed. Conversely, climate scientists are attempting to understand the factors that would precipitate a range of possible futures, from best-case scenarios for carbon emission reductions to worst-case predictions that result in such dramatic increases in extreme weather conditions that much of the world becomes a barren wasteland akin to that in George Miller's 1979 classic film *Mad Max*.[3] Thus, it would be prudent to carefully consider the potential for dystopian outcomes while thinking about highly desirable, even utopian futures.

The word 'utopia' was coined by Thomas More, and used as the title for his 1561 work of socio-political satirical fiction.[4] Published in Latin, the book's subtitle translates to '*On the Best State of a Commonwealth and on the New Island of Utopia, A Truly Golden Handbook, No Less Beneficial than Entertaining*'. However, the etymology of the word derives not from Latin but from ancient Greek: οὐ ('not') and τόπος ('place') thus meaning no-place, which might be More's admission that it cannot exist in the real world. Its antonym, 'dystopia', literally means 'bad place'.

More's *Utopia*, a blend of reality and fiction, describes a provocative alternative reality of Tudor England; a perfect nation of 54 nearly identical cities surrounded by farmland on a roughly circular island, where no city may have more than 6,000 residents, family size is controlled, work is important but limited to six hours a day, and idleness is a punishable offence. Gold is devalued, used for chamber pots and worn by slaves; healthcare is universal; property, possessions and resources, including food, are communal and all citizens must take turns participating in farming labour, living a mix of rural and urban life. While there is much freedom of choice for citizens, men

Ambrosius Holbein, *The Island of Utopia (Thomas More's Utopia)*, 1518

Holbein's woodcutting shows a bird's-eye view of Thomas More's *Utopia*. The crescent-shaped island is 322 kilometres (200 miles) wide, encompassing 54 cities separated by 38-kilometre (24-mile) wide green belts, with the capital Amaurotum at the centre. Each city-state is roughly square shaped, with each side at least 32 kilometres (20 miles) long.

Mingjia Shi and Yichen Sheng, The Garden of Earthly Delights, Parametric Parasite CDE design studio, Melbourne School of Design, University of Melbourne, 2022

This project for a speculative design studio proposes a vision for a possible future urban environment by introducing bees en masse into Barcelona. The speculative vision dynamically changes its character between dystopia and utopia – a future led by machines to find a new garden of earthly delights suitable for the present and ready for the future. Studio leaders: Justyna Karakiewicz and Liang Yang.

and women all wear the same clothes, only distinguished by genders; people's movement is subject to strictly enforced rules and all must live 'in full view', so no one can break a rule undetected. Many of More's concepts have been influential not only in philosophy and political theory, but also in speculative city design, such as cities with capped population sizes, agricultural green belts, urban and rural lifestyles, communal food production and consumption, and forays into the provision of urban health, safety, wellbeing and unity through observation and surveillance. These themes are explored in this issue of △. While much of More's *Utopia* was a positive provocation in the context of 1500s Tudor England, many of the book's themes, such as communal living, slavery and lifetime leaders, became core ingredients of the dystopias that would follow.

An early dystopian exploration can be found in Jonathan Swift's *Gulliver's Travels* (1726), in which he identified European society's socio-political trends and extrapolated them to satirical extremes, exposing their underlying flaws. Gulliver, the book's protagonist, visits cities that initially appear impressive and wonderful but upon closer inspection turn out to be deeply problematic. One of these is the Flying Island of Laputa, a technocratic marvel run by a highly educated elite that developed multidirectional magnetic levitation transportation for the city similar in concept to the Shanghai maglev train (2004). The city floats above the ground-dwelling underclass and can be moved to block their sunlight – a thinly veiled criticism of English rule over Ireland. Unlike in science fiction, where the impossible, such as time travel or defying gravity, is posited as fact for the purpose of the narrative, literature about the objectively real possible – a category of literature commonly termed 'speculative fiction' – makes us aware that right now we already have all the ingredients for certain urban futures.

A collective wrong decision is all that is needed to propel society towards an oppressive patriarchal religious dystopia such as that described by Canadian author Margaret Atwood in *The Handmaid's Tale* (1985).[5] The writer describes a far-right Christian takeover of the US (now Gilead), a dark response to loss of fertility, food shortages and a contamination crisis. The story cuts close to the bone in light of events such as the Capitol Riots (2021)[6] and the overturning of Roe v Wade in the US (2022),[7] and Atwood's speculative fiction gives us a clear indication of where this politico-religious trend may go if allowed to continue, while providing hope that it is not too late for us to reverse the direction in which we are heading.

For a brighter world, society must question what sorts of cities are wanted. Optimistic speculations, including the 'probable' and utopian 'possible' propositions, need not be top-down visions but must provide projections for a plurality of futures. Putting forward and exploring dystopic fiction that incorporates speculative design builds an understanding of the slight forks in the path towards a better future, and an understanding of the urban design strategies and technologies that, if adopted and adapted, may lead to disturbing and potentially damaging outcomes.

JJ Grandville,
Flying island of Laputa from Gulliver's Travels,
Realm of Balnibarbi east of Japan,
1856

Grandville's etching depicting Jonathan Swift's 7-kilometre (4.5-mile) wide Flying Island of Laputa. The island can be manoeuvred in any direction using magnetic levitation developed by its scientifically educated but impractical elite ruling class. Balnibarbi is the country where the underclass live, below Laputa and controlled by it using threats to pelt the inhabitants with large stones or cut off sunlight and rain.

The Country into the City, or the City into the Country?

The first group of articles in this issue address, in very diverse ways, dichotomies of city and country, built urban fabric and parks, access to nature, food, and ocular-centric control versus eco-centric coevolution. The challenge of feeding the world will remain ongoing as long as population continues to expand. While cities have grown on the strength of surplus agricultural production, leaving that increasingly efficient and mechanised production outside the city walls, the impacts of agriculture and food transport on carbon emissions and world ecology suggest the need for speculation about subverting or reversing that relationship. Daniele Belleri and Carlo Ratti explore the extent to which in-city agriculture is a romance, the answer to a prayer, or a risky pathway to increased corporatisation and food insecurity. Blurring the dichotomy between city and country still further, Justyna Karakiewicz explores these environmental issues by leaving behind the anthropocentric view of settlement in favour of dynamic adaptive coevolution between human development and interacting natural processes.

Frank Lloyd Wright's Broadacre City concept – the idealisation of the mid-20th-century suburb – presented in his book *The Disappearing City* (1932)[8] – has subsequently lost some of its currency since the environmental impact of human greed for living space, now incorporated into the concept of our carbon footprint, has begun to have noticeable and disastrous effects worldwide. But global pandemic lockdowns, intended to physically isolate people from one another, spurred a surge in virtual social interaction and digital commerce. Marcus White and Stephen Glackin investigate what living in a 'Broadband-acre City' looks like now and for the speculative future far beyond our current era. Ebenezer Howard's Garden City (1902) adopted a concentric plan to increase access to green urban 'lungs' for housing and social and commercial areas. Nano Langenheim and Kongjian Yu muse on whether his rigid geometrical schema can be shaken up for the 21st-century relationship between human habitation and broader ecological interests or, conversely, whether this might lead to increasing clashes with non-human predators.

In the modern era, the city as a landscape has been fundamentally influenced by the parterres of 15th- and 16th-century French formal gardens via the Beaux-Arts architectural movement (1830s–1870s) and its interpretation by the City Beautiful movement in the US, lasting from the 1890s to the early 1900s. The grand urban gestures and vistas, designed to be seen from above and experienced from the perspective of foot traffic and carriages, gave way to other forms of architecture, experienced from an aerial perspective and designed with different priorities, during the 20th and 21st centuries. Jordi Oliveras charts this journey to the aerotropolis and visual 'selfie city' of today and beyond.

Urban Heat, Movement, Social Divisions and Surveillance

The next group of articles consider questions of problematic urban microclimates, and how these can or might be addressed in the future. Specific philosophical, design and structural decisions underlie the impact of the contemporary urban fabric on carbon emissions, exacerbated social and income disparities, social unrest, surveillance and security practices. These decisions and results are considered and extrapolated to explore where they may lead.

Luke Kim, Arinah Rizal and Qun Zhang,
Diversity through Disruption design elective,
Melbourne School of Design, University of
Melbourne with Los Andes University,
Bogota,
2020

The project explores dynamic adaptive coevolution and the potential of new manufacturing technologies where, instead of using AI-controlled drones for surveillance or military strikes, they are used for weaving nets for recreational activities and natural structures. The project was part of a course examining complex adaptive systems, human development and natural processes. Coordinator: Justyna Karakiewicz.

Nano Langenheim,
An Eco-dystopic Urban Forest,
Melbourne, Australia,
2022

An exploration of an overgrown 'rewilded' urban rejuvenation project where a well-intended desire for a 'city in the forest' has backfired, resulting in neither an operational city nor a biologically functioning forest. The project represents a 'mid-journey' destruction of both the forest and the city.

Paolo Soleri,
Infrababel, original drawing,
1968-9

Utopian architect Soleri coined the term 'arcology' to describe the fusion of architecture with ecology. This conceptual design was to be located in a stone quarry. Designed for a population of 100,000, it is one of a series of environmentally driven designs by Soleri, who also founded and commenced the development of the utopian community of Arcosanti in the Arizona desert (1970–).

Most contemporary cities have a partially subterranean mirror city. Its extent depends on many factors – size and underlying geology perhaps first among them. However, as the world focuses more on resilience and defensive approaches to destructive and inhospitable climatic extremes, the opportunities of going underground become more manifest, comprehensive and widespread. Jane Burry and Mehrnoush Latifi use Paolo Soleri's influential, speculative and partially realised future Arcological cities (1970) as a stepping-off point to ponder the utopian and dystopian realities of building and living underground.

Marcus White and Tianyi Yang extend this approach towards mitigating the effects of climate change to reconsider Le Corbusier's proposition for Ville Radieuse (1933). While the widely spaced grid of towers was conceived in a park-like setting to address air quality and green views, it might also present a way to address the problem of urban heat islands in densely packed, rapidly overheating cities. Like thermal comfort, frictionless mobility has played a huge part in cities becoming both bloated carbon emitters and, in some aspects, less than hospitable and healthy. Ian Woodcock considers the potential pros and cons for the nature of cities in a future world of autonomous electric mobility. Tridib Banerjee explores a city that was 'smart' before the era of smart cities, and how it has taken on the contemporary smart-city mantle. In particular, he uncovers Chandigarh's underlying postcolonial roots and the insidious way in which its urban structure has reinforced and even exacerbated social division. Andong Lu transports us from Jane Jacobs' sense of a safer city with eyes on the street – local citizens engaged in and observing their immediate environs – to the ways that cybertracking, fixed camera and mobile surveillance are changing the city and concepts of privacy. Crime protection or state threat? Where is this trend heading and how is it likely to influence the city far into the future?

Zoning, Linearity, Floating and Organic City Planning

The articles mentioned above demonstrate many of the forces shaping cities and their potential future impacts. The final articles investigate the overall physical form and distribution of the city, whilst being driven by very different sets of underlying

Marcus White/Harrison and White and Tianyi Yang,
Digital rendering of
Le Corbusier's 1930 Ville Radieuse
(Radiant City),
2022

Though criticised widely, Le Corbusier's Radiant City urban design proposal of a series of high-rise mixed-use towers surrounded by generous green spaces provides high levels of daylight amenity for occupants. Due to the scheme's high levels of sky view factor across the entire city, it would allow longwave radiation to escape to the atmosphere and would therefore be exceptionally well suited to mitigating the urban heat island effect.

Yueyao Li, Fungi Punk and Future Mycelium Cities, Parametric Parasite CDE design studio, Melbourne School of Design, University of Melbourne, 2022

The project explores a disastrous future. Sea-level rise devours cities on the coastline, human-built environments collapse, but a fungal colony survives and serves as the new foundation for the city to re-emerge. Matured mycelium structures turn to city transportation systems, habitats and subterranean spaces. Studio leaders: Justyna Karakiewicz and Liang Yang.

concepts. Tony Garnier's visionary urban plan Cité Industrielle (1900s) largely set the agenda for modernist city zoning in the 20th century, decisively separating industrial activity from housing, social activity and local commerce. Its influence has endured through two subsequent industrial revolutions. Jane Burry questions the place of Garnier's zoning in the seemingly placeless, seamlessly digital world of Industry 4.0.

A powerful idea coming from Ivan Leonidov's Magnitogorsk (1930) is the concept of the linear city. Kas Oosterhuis reflects on a career of environmentally driven ideas for cities and questions whether the time is right for Magnitogorsk to return in the guise of the new city of NEOM in Saudi Arabia. Cities are shaped by topography; sometimes when the land runs out, they take to the water. Dan Nyandega uncovers the optimistic and less-optimistic futures for Makoko, an informal floating settlement on Lagos Lagoon in Nigeria. Claudia Pasquero and Marco Poletto's article is a fully speculative return to nature to uncover the optimal form for the city, deploying data to investigate bio-digital futures and living with what English philosopher and ecologist Timothy Morton has called 'strange strangers'.[9]

While this issue of 𝐃 explores dystopic possibilities for the future of cities, it also offers hope. What drives us forward, as German social philosopher Ernst Bloch noted in *The Principle of Hope* (1986),[10] are optimistic daydreams of a better, brighter world. Bloch identified utopias and visions of fulfilment as motivational elements of radical social change, because we need to be able to see things differently to be able to change them. Utopian escapism might be the seed required for a new and more humane social order, and bottom-up utopias are an 'immature, but an honest substitute for revolution'.[11] 𝐃

Notes
1. Oscar Wilde, 'The Soul of Man under Socialism', *Fortnightly Review*, February 1891, p 292.
2. Anthony Dunne and Fiona Raby, *Speculative Everything: Design, Fiction, and Social Dreaming*, MIT Press (Cambridge, MA), 2013, p 224.
3. George Miller, *Mad Max* (film), Roadshow Film Distributors, Australia, 1979.
4. Thomas More, *Utopia: On the Best State of a Commonwealth and On the New Island of Utopia; A Truly Golden Handbook, No Less Beneficial than Entertaining*, William Bulmer/Shakespeare Press (London), 1808, originally published in 1516.
5. Margaret Atwood, *The Handmaid's Tale*, McClelland and Stewart (Toronto), 1985.
6. Brenna M Davidson and Tetsuro Kobayashi, 'The Effect of Message Modality on Memory for Political Disinformation: Lessons from the 2021 US Capitol Riots', *Computers in Human Behavior*, 132 (107241), January 2022, pp 2, 3.
7. Dan Mangan and Kevin Breuninger, 'Supreme Court Overturns Roe v Wade, Ending 50 Years of Federal Abortion Rights', 24 June 2022: www.cnbc.com/2022/06/24/roe-v-wade-overturned-by-supreme-court-ending-federal-abortion-rights.html.
8. William Farquhar Payson, *The Disappearing City by Frank Lloyd Wright*, Stratford Press (New York), 1932.
9. Timothy Morton, 'The Mesh', *Environmental Criticism for the Twenty-First Century*, Routledge (Abingdon), 2011, p 19.
10. Ernst Bloch and Neville Plaice, *The Principle Of Hope*, Vol 3, MIT Press (Cambridge, MA), 1986.
11. *Ibid*, p 368.

Text © 2023 John Wiley & Sons Ltd. Images: pp 6–7 © Kundi Shu, Kachung Lo and Xiufeng Li; pp 8–9(b) © Mingjia Shi and Yichen Sheng; pp 10–11(c) © Luke Kim, Arinah Rizal and Qun Zhang; p 11(tr) © Nano Langenheim; p 11(br) © Cosanti Foundation; pp 12–13(t) Yueyao Li; pp 12–13(b) © Marcus White/Harrison and White and Tianyi Yang

URBAN FARMING

AeroFarms,
Newark, New Jersey,
2021

Farming systems such as the one used by AeroFarms' production plant – one of the largest aeroponic indoor vertical farms of its kind – aim to grow fruit and vegetables using up to 95 per cent less water and zero pesticides while employing artificial intelligence to monitor the status of crops.

Daniele Belleri and Carlo Ratti

THE RELUCTANT UTOPIA

The old conceptual dichotomy between the city and the countryside has often been a historical stumbling block for architects and urban planners. Whilst there have been many attempts to bring the city closer to the natural environment, some on grand scales, more modest experiments have often gleaned better results. **Daniele Belleri** is a partner at design and innovation office CRA-Carlo Ratti Associati, where he is in charge of all editorial and curatorial projects. He and the practice's founder, architect and engineer **Carlo Ratti** – who is director of the Senseable City Lab at the Massachusetts Institute of Technology (MIT) – together explore our contemporary options.

If the UN's demographic forecast holds true, an extra 2.5 billion individuals will join the global dinner table by 2050.[1] Feeding the growing urban masses will be an extraordinary challenge amidst the convulsions of climate change, and both the Covid-19 pandemic and Russia's invasion of Ukraine remind us that international supply chains are only as strong as their weakest links.

At the core of this challenge is the conceptual wall we have built between the city, the countryside and food. Cities were born around 10,000 years ago, when agriculture yielded surplus food and increasing opportunities for professional specialisation. Ultimately, great masses of people came together, and the crops were left outside. In the following millennia, technological innovations allowed an ever-smaller number of farmers to feed the rest of the world, crowded into cities. Now, as we reckon with the multiple threats of our anthropocenic present, we cannot follow the old urbanisation playbook so uncritically. Perhaps it is time to bring food production into cities; perhaps urban agriculture can feed a new urban utopia.

Staying Away from the City

Because the dichotomy between city and countryside is so rigid, few utopian thinkers have entertained urban agriculture as an ingredient for a better world. Many of the utopias of the last two centuries have been about extending the city towards the countryside without contemplating the other direction. Consider Ebenezer Howard's Garden City in the UK at the turn of the 19th century or Broadacre City by Frank Lloyd Wright in the 1930s US. These schemes involved stretching the city into country-like aesthetics while not paying much attention to the vital activity of agriculture in everyday life. Others have imagined farming itself as a key, but also abandoned the city entirely – take, for example, the French phalanstery or the Jewish kibbutz. In the 2020 Guggenheim Museum exhibition 'Countryside: A Report', Rem Koolhaas and AMO framed the countryside as 'the remaining 98% of the earth's surface',[2] reproposing the dichotomy that keeps the city and the countryside separate.

One can argue that farming has mostly played a peripheral role in the urban imagination. It has emerged in times of crisis, and it evokes tragic scarcity more often than utopian abundance. In American cities, think of 1890 Detroit's Pingree's Potato Patches, a municipal government initiative providing unemployed workers with vacant lots to be turned into community gardens;[3] or the Victory Gardens of the First and Second World Wars that boosted morale on the home front by giving people a self-directed way to contribute to the war effort. Amidst the ruins of post-1945 Europe, starving citizens converted parts of central parks and squares – from Berlin's Tiergarten to Milan's Piazza del Duomo – into crop fields. Later on, the US financial crises of the 1970s caused decentralised, grassroots community gardens to begin appearing across Lower Manhattan. These 'Green Guerrillas' inspired counterparts globally, adding to a history of urban farming that is far from the value of planned urban utopias.

Victory Garden, Washington DC, 1943

The Victory Gardens initiative spread across US cities during both the First and Second World Wars when American presidents called on their compatriots to plant vegetable gardens to ward off any possible threat of food shortages.

Tech Experiments and a Product Listing Mag

Since the 1960s, a series of cultural products and scientific experiments have begun to establish urban farming as more than a marginal or provisional practice. Some of the artefacts of this period seem unlikely venues for utopian representations of farming, but nonetheless played a crucial role. The *Whole Earth Catalog* was an independent product-listing magazine issued in California in the late 1960s and early 1970s. Focused on self-sufficiency and read by 'communards and other participants in the back-to-the-land movement',[4] it mostly advocated an ex-urban type of communitarianism. However, it also paved the way for an encounter between entrepreneurialism, environmental conscience and technological avant-gardism – from early cybernetic theories to the coeval visions of Richard Buckminster Fuller – that underpinned several urban farming experiments of the following decades.

In parallel to these evolving cultural discourses, scientists across the world were experimenting with new food-cultivation technologies to create self-sustaining communities, even in outer space. From 1991 to 1993, Biosphere 2 in Arizona brought eight people to live inside a three-acre, sealed ecological dome, where they were expected to be reliant on the food they were growing inside. However, the means of production of this early 'food bubble' turned out to be insufficient: the participants, while not falling into malnutrition, did not produce quite enough calories for themselves.[5] Few utopias dance to the tune of rumbling stomachs.

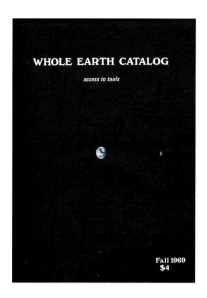

Cover of the *Whole Earth Catalog*, Fall 1969

One of the most influential countercultural magazines of its period, the *Whole Earth Catalog* was focused on providing readers with the tools to achieve self-sufficiency. This included a focus on agricultural tools and methods that individuals could employ on a relatively small scale.

Biosphere 2 campus and museum, Oracle, Arizona, 1989

The exterior of Biosphere 2, a closed geodesic dome where experiments in the late 20th century attempted to create a self-sustaining environment. Today, the University of Arizona uses the facility for a variety of research applications.

Instead, the most important innovations possibly arose from humbler research into alternative farming methods. Consider aeroponics, which started in the Netherlands during the 1950s and became commercially available to a wider audience in the 1980s. It allows plants to be grown without soil, their roots suspended in the air. We have also seen advances in hydroponics, which allows plants to be grown in water. Aquaponics, which has precedent with the *chinampas* of the Aztecs, merges hydroponics with the cultivation of fish. These new systems enable a whole range of sophisticated integrations between farms and cities. French botanist Patrick Blanc's vertical gardens, which spread internationally as part of designs such as Herzog & de Meuron's Caixa Forum in Madrid (2007) or CRA-Carlo Ratti Associati's Trussardi Dehors in Milan (2008), are strictly connected with the new possibilities brought forward by hydroponics.

CRA-Carlo Ratti Associati,
Trussardi Dehors,
Milan,
2008

One of the first vertical garden projects in Europe, the project features a set of 120 plant species selected by French botanist Patrick Blanc, all of them placed on a thin support structure, creating the effect of a green cloud floating in space.

CRA-Carlo Ratti Associati,
Jian Mu Tower,
Shenzhen, China,
2022

The project features more than 10,000 square metres (107,640 square feet) of space dedicated to the cultivation of crops, aiming to produce enough food to sustain all inhabitants and users of the skyscraper. The prominence of greenery on the building's surface also reduces solar irradiance in indoor areas and the need for air conditioning.

The 218-metre (715-foot) high building, designed for Chinese supermarket chain Wumart, features a façade that doubles as vertical farming infrastructure. The hydroponic system was developed in collaboration with Italian agritech company ZERO Farms.

Pairing these new technologies with an environmental conscience, we can envision a trajectory towards a new design utopia. Instead of extending the city back into nature – resulting in the folly of suburban sprawl – our challenge is to bring nature back into the city. Public opinion, increasingly aware of the climate crisis and its gravity, can help push city officials to start the process, including with urban agriculture.

Designers across the world are starting to rethink how agriculture could be embedded within the heart of the city. They are experimenting with new architectural languages and functions, from skyscrapers where the façades can be used to produce crops for local inhabitants – such as the Jian Mu Tower CRA designed for the city of Shenzhen in 2022 in collaboration with agritech company ZERO Farms – to converting city parks into productive agricultural landscapes. It is also necessary to consider how governments can supercharge existing peripheral urban agriculture, vastly expanding capacity for bottom-up community gardens.

Moreover, within indoor farms, a host of new technologies can reinvent agriculture as we know it. Robots, surgically tending to a diversity of plants that the brute force of a tractor or a crop duster hardly could, might help us leave monoculture behind. Optimisations for lighting, soil content, and water use – powered by big data – could vastly reduce the environmental cost of every crop we grow.

In the last few years, numerous startups have emerged, failed and emerged again with a focus on indoor farming. Though often located in large metropolitan areas, they have avoided the heavy costs of real estate in a city centre. Bowery Farming and AeroFarms near New York, Paris' Agricool, Berlin's InFarm, Dubai's CropOne and Hong Kong's Farm66 – these projects have earned media interest and genuine hopes for their high-tech agricultural visions. However, the long-term economic viability of these businesses remains uncertain.

Lest It Would Not Be Too Successful

The do-it-yourself appeal of urban agriculture faces steep challenges as it scales up, emergent properties that could spin out of control into disasters and dystopias. Could urban agriculture go the same way as the Internet, where an initially excited, independent spirit could rapidly give way to big corporations using data, technology and market power to irresponsibly control the entire sector? Because new mechanisms of urban agriculture have high startup costs and demand high levels of expertise, we could face yet another futuristic dream that becomes our next monopolistic nightmare. Smelling an opportunity, tech companies are building vegetable factories across the world. If we want to make the most of urban agriculture, governments should get ahead of their disruptive innovations and prepare to regulate the sector for the good of citizens. The alternative dystopia might be the ultimate corporatisation of urban farming, which critics warn is already underway.[6]

> Tech companies are building vegetable factories across the world. If we want to make the most of urban agriculture, governments should get ahead of their disruptive innovations and prepare to regulate the sector for the good of citizens. The alternative dystopia might be the ultimate corporatisation of urban farming, which critics warn is already underway

For example, a substantial issue derives from the lack of natural light in cities, which forces agritech companies to use artificial lighting on a wide scale. So even if local farming helps save on energy for transportation and local delivery, a disproportionate amount of energy to replace that of the sun would end up being consumed.

Another great advantage of urban agriculture – the incorporation of technology ranging from big data to robots – also entails a deadly vulnerability to technological errors or malicious hacking. If urban farming became overly successful, so as to render urban dwellers fully reliant on it for their food supply, our cities would become dangerously vulnerable to ransomware. Moreover, bringing a large percentage of overall food production into the urban core would put more of humanity's eggs into a single basket; a single siege or natural disaster would disrupt not only people and traditional urban economic activity, but food production itself. After all, the case was made that suburban planning in the postwar US should be pursued precisely to reduce the country's exposure in the event of a nuclear attack by the Soviet Union.[7] America has no one city that would cost itself, but France would crumble rapidly if a bomb fell on Paris.

Luckily, these most serious risks can be addressed with a commitment to diversification where no one company or monolithic technology set should dominate the business, and traditional, rural farming should remain a critical source of our food (few propose otherwise). These reservations remind us that urban agriculture is not a panacea. It is instead an exciting new ingredient in the complex recipe to feed the world, one that will take time to balance with the flavour of others.

Feeding a Wider Utopia?

Urban farming is just one technology, and has distinctly limited horizons. However, it has grander possibilities if it can help teach us to reconcile the natural and artificial. The utopia that our century demands is one in which humans develop a new relationship with the natural world; the dystopia that looms is one in which our species and our planet destroy each other. Urban farming could be one step that brings the natural and artificial closer together, and gives us the fuel to begin taking the others. As billions of people pour from the countryside into our cities, it is critical that we invite parts of the countryside they came from – especially the plants and the soil – to come with them.

New possibilities for urban agriculture give us a chance to break down the dualism between cities and the organic worlds that sustain them. In 1938, American urban historian Lewis Mumford invited his readers to rethink the image of the medieval city, which was 'not merely a vital social environment: it was likewise adequate … on the biological side. There were smoky rooms to endure; but there was also perfume in the garden behind the burgher's house… the odor of flowering orchards in the spring, or the scent of the new mown hay, floating across the fields in early summer.'[8] Can we recognise that even today, our cities are more alive than we believe them to be?

ZERO Farms,
Pordenone, Italy,
2021

Agritech company ZERO Farms pursues a business model that combines aeroponic cultivation – completely avoiding the use of soil or other substrates – with urban redevelopment. It has developed a modular construction system that allows it to mass-produce vertical farms within old or disused industrial spaces.

Notes
1. United Nations Department of Economic and Social Affairs, *World Urbanization Prospects: The 2018 Revision*, United Nations (New York), 2019, p 9: https://population.un.org/wup/Publications/Files/WUP2018-Report.pdf.
2. Rem Koolhaas, *Countryside: A Report*, Taschen (Cologne), 2020, p 5.
3. 'Grown from the Past: A Short History of Community Gardening in the United States': https://communityofgardens.si.edu/exhibits/show/historycommunitygardens/vacantlot#:~:text=The%20first%20community%20gardens%20in,vacant%20lots%20in%20the%20city.
4. Anna Wiener, 'The Complicated Legacy of Stewart Brand's "Whole Earth Catalog"', *The New Yorker*, 16 November 2018: www.newyorker.com/news/letter-from-silicon-valley/the-complicated-legacy-of-stewart-brands-whole-earth-catalog.
5. David Sinclair and Matthew D LaPlante, *Lifespan: Why We Age – and Why We Don't Have To*, Thorsons (London), 2019, p 92.
6. Kim Severson, 'No Soil. No Growing Seasons. Just Add Water and Technology', *The New York Times*, 6 July 2021: www.nytimes.com/2021/07/06/dining/hydroponic-farming.html.
7. Richard Pommer, David Spaeth and Kevin Harrington (eds), *In the Shadow of Mies: Ludwig Hilberseimer – Architect, Educator, and Urban Planner*, The Art Institute of Chicago and Rizzoli International Publications (New York and Chicago), 1988, pp 89–93.
8. Lewis Mumford, *The Culture of Cities*, Harcourt Brace & Company (New York), 1938, p 49.

Text © 2023 John Wiley & Sons Ltd. Images: pp 14-15 © AeroFarms; p 16 Library of Congress, Prints & Photographs Division, FSA/OWI Collection, [LC-DIG-fsa-8d29785]; p 17(b) © University of Arizona; p 18 © CRA-Carlo Ratti Associati, photo Pino dell'Aquila; p 19 © CRA-Carlo Ratti Associati; pp 20–1 © ZERO Farms

PER TOP

Speculative Thinking in

Justyna Karakiewicz

Shi Percy Pan, Yingna Celina Sun and Jiaao Wayne Wong,
The Great Ocean Road is Crying in Tears of Plastic,
Studio 05, Melbourne School of Design,
University of Melbourne, Australia,
2021

Speculation on a possible future. How might our future look if we do not stop producing plastic?

LA
a Short-Term World

In the face of climate change and human equity, architects are still presenting pristine images of perfect urban plans stuck in the aspic of a bygone age that has precipitated the difficult global condition we find ourselves in. Here **Justyna Karakiewicz** – Professor of Architecture and Urban Design in the Faculty of Architecture, Building and Planning at the University of Melbourne – describes some of the conceptual and practical notions explored at her home university to ameliorate this.

Ambrogio Lorenzetti,
The Allegory of God and Bad Government,
1338–9

Two of six scenes depicted in the three-panel fresco in Siena's Town Hall in Tuscany representing the consequences of 'good' and 'bad' government reflected in the city structure and surrounding countryside.

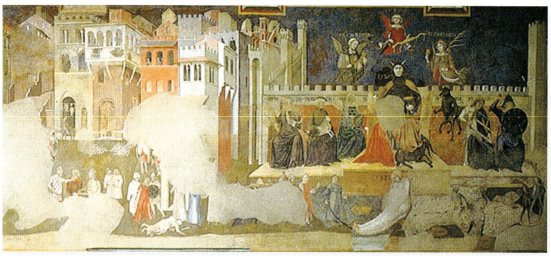

The six fresco panels of Ambrogio Lorenzetti's *The Allegory of Good and Bad Government* (1338–9) in Siena's Town Hall in Tuscany are a clear illustration of utopia and dystopia. Here the dialectic is set out for all to fear. Yet this is a false dialectic; we do not exist in one of the two polar conditions posited, the unattainable or the undesirable. Instead, our urban reality exists between the two, in the realm of 'pertopia' or 'perturbanism', in a constant unstable and evolving realm of disruption and reconstitution, of optimism and potential. Contemporary images also seek to induce change through fear of the future. In Shi Pan, Yinga Sun and Jiaao Wong's 2021 student project *The Great Ocean Road is Crying in Tears of Plastic*, the future is not one engaged through desire, but fear.

Likewise, in Pieter Bruegel the Elder's *Tower of Babel* (1563), we see the tower finished in part, ruined in part and also under construction. When viewing this image, we can narrate a thousand stories of different futures, some bad and some good. Using contemporary technologies, we could today create many depictions using parametrically controlled modelling to explore these different futures and perhaps even postulate 'what if?'.

Unfortunately, instead we are frequently beguiled and teased by alluring images produced by architects, urban designers and planners, where everything is just perfect, if not wholly realistic. These images portray perfect scenarios for a perfect future. Photorealistic perspectives depict a sky that is always blue, where everything is clean and perfect, where all the people are immaculately dressed, and where there are no unsavoury individuals or thoughts. With everything resolved, there are no dilapidating buildings or buildings under construction. Life is frozen in one perfect moment. We sell these images to our clients, and some of them still live under the illusion that this is possible. And it does not matter if our vision for this perfection (often labelled as a sustainable future) is located in the suburbs or in a dense compact city – we still repeat the same utopian mistakes. These perfect frozen futures are untenable because they are conceived by the same fallacious decisions and thought patterns that led to the situations we are trying to address.

If we want to move towards a more sustainable way of life, we cannot believe in frozen dreams, since sustainability depends on change, flexibility and adaptability. What is sustainable today will not be sustainable tomorrow. But above all, we can no longer create futures that are totally preoccupied only with human beings. Anthropocentric design has no place. As Sim Van der Ryn and Stuart Cowan elegantly point out: 'We have used design very cleverly in the service of narrowly defined human interests but have neglected its relationship with our fellow creatures.'[1]

A similar idea comes from Michael Neuman in his 'The Compact City Fallacy' (2005), in which he points out that instead of repeating our mistakes, we should 'raise the level of the game' and not remain 'on the same playing field' by means of a co-evolutionary process.[2]

But can we still indulge in slow evolutionary processes, where changes are happening gradually and often remain unnoticed and do not therefore unsettle us or make us think differently. Furthermore, as Jonathan Rowson of the Social

Pieter Bruegel the Elder,
The Tower of Babel,
1563

Bruegel's image can be read as an example of a pertopian vision. Nothing is certain, nothing is perfected; the world awaits additions and subtractions. Looking at this picture, we can speculate on possible futures, write a thousand different stories and model the consequences of our decisions.

Brain Centre at the Royal Society of Arts in London points out, we have great difficulty forming new and positive habits and keeping them.[3] He also observes that changing our context is a more powerful way of shaping our behaviour than trying to change our mind. But to what extent are we able to change our context. And are we, as human beings, only truly motivated when something shakes up our comfortable existence and leads us to desire something that we perceive we lack.[4]

Changing Our Conceptual Framework

At the Melbourne School of Design at the University of Melbourne, work on perturbanism and pertopian propositions began in 2013, in the Galapagos Islands, with annual month-long intensive workshops for students. The students were required to abandon their preconceptions that humans are constantly under threat from nature and need to fight back with design, and asked to forget urban theories in which deterministic progressions are privileged. In place of these, complex adaptive system (CAS) theory, which postulates that any healthy system requires periodic perturbation, was adopted. In this context, a perturbation is understood as deviation of a system from its initial state by internal or external stimuli. The external stimuli in urban form can be achieved through interventions, but we know that the interventions act on emergent qualities of the system that are unpredictable, so by definition they are not foreseen or planned.

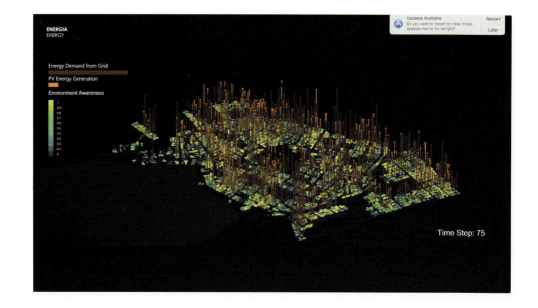

Justyna Karakiewicz,
Modelling consequences
of perturbations,
Urban Galapagos research project,
Melbourne School of Design,
University of Melbourne,
Australia,
2018

Phyton 3x with an object-oriented programming structure was used to model the consequences of perturbations (the installation of photovoltaic panels and piezoelectrics) on city structure and environmental awareness among the residents.

The Galapagos Islands were the original laboratory for this research as students needed to recognise that design interventions are a part of larger systems and cannot be conceived solely for the benefit of humans

The enquiry into perturbanism is not a problem-solving exercise or a search for resolved solutions; instead, a perturbation enables further and consequent change. In the terminology of CAS theory, this is a change that could result in evolution or revolution.

The Galapagos Islands were the original laboratory for this research as students needed to recognise that design interventions are a part of larger systems and cannot be conceived solely for the benefit of humans. Here they could observe how humans exert influence on resources, and how human activities have a profound impact on the environment that cannot be mitigated by superficial strategies.

However, with the pandemic constraints on travel in 2020, it was necessary to find something closer to Melbourne. It became clear that the Great Ocean Road in Victoria is suffering from many similar issues to those in the Galapagos. The name of the road itself reflects an attitude that human activity dominates. As the coast is threatened by erosion and rising sea levels, the role of the road demands reconsideration and a reassessment of our value systems and cultural priorities. This thread of asphalt is symptomatic of a crisis, not only for its purpose of connection, but also for its priorities. The road is a representation of our conundrums. Extensive evidence increasingly calls for recognition of the urban and natural ecosystems as continuities, not disjuncture. From the CAS perspective, urban form can be considered as part of the natural system to contribute to a better quality of life for all species; that is, turning our focus from 'people-centric' to 'life-centric' development for all of nature.

In our current circumstances, we appear to cling to the hope that technology will rescue us from the catastrophe that it has wrought. But isn't it what we can now call the technosphere (everything that is developed or modified by humans using new technologies) that is leading us into continuous destruction? As Mitch Mignano observes in 'Harmony of the Spheres' (2003), the only way to stop this and transform it into continuous creation is through harmony in the biosphere and noosphere; that is, in our norms and value systems.[5]

Perturbanism is not the urban design equivalent of 'chicken soup', the preparation of something that is easy to digest and comforting. Instead, any perturbation should provoke us to see things in a different light, and perhaps to start thinking differently. If this perturbation can demonstrate an attractive consequence, such as financial profit or improved quality of life, then the idea could be accepted and replicated elsewhere, leading to changes of norms and values within the noosphere and, hence, policies.

This design approach is partially a search for urban negentropy, so the first step in any project is to find the entropy within the system. Once the location of the energy loss within a social or urban system is identified, we prioritise the losses and develop a plan of action for a scenario. When building this scenario, we ensure that feedback loops, essential for the complex adaptive system to work, are clearly understood. Using an agent-based model, the impact of the perturbation in the urban structure is examined. The proposals are then tested and modified iteratively until a reasonable outcome is postulated.

In their Rhizomic Bridge project, students Kundi Shu, Ka Chung Lo and Xiufeng Li looked at the possible consequences of coastal erosion and the loss of land over the next 300 years. If this erosion occurs, bridges will need to be constructed to maintain connections between local communities. The entropy in this, the energy lost in the social and urban system, was noted. However, the negative consequences of constructing a bridge by further disturbing the marine ecology could lead to more entropic behaviour. The challenge, therefore, was to build a bridge that could have a positive effect on the environment and also on the social system.

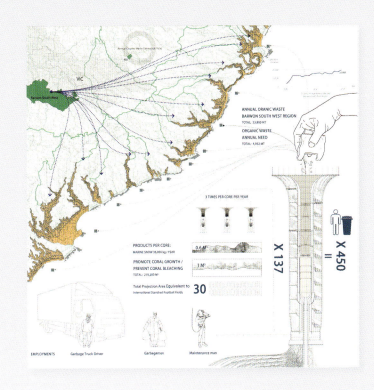

The consequences of coastal erosion along the Great Ocean Road over the next 300 years, based on demographic and Geoscience Digital Earth Australia Coastlines data.

```
Kundi Shu, Ka Chung Lo and Xiufeng Li,
Rhizomic Bridge,
Studio 05,
Melbourne School of Design,
University of Melbourne, Australia,
2021
```

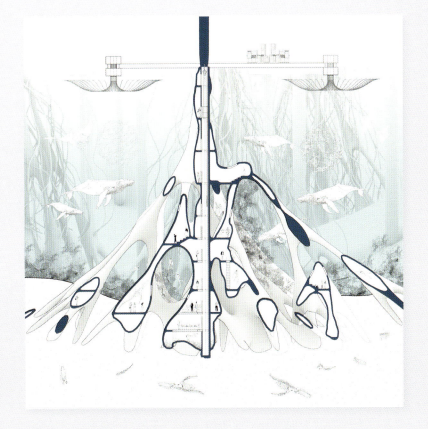

Initial perturbation in the form of thin bridge pylons and platforms used for deliveries of organic waste. The pylons are placed in specific locations to promote coral growth around them. This is achieved by the introduction of the marine snow produced from organic waste, and will help to stabilise the seabed and slow down coastal erosion.

Filtering, Separation, and Spraying Device
01. Supernatants after Second-Precipitation
02. Semi-permeable Membrane Filtration
03. High-speed Separator
04. Marine Snow Hydraulic Injector
05. Swings Pipes with the Inner Airflow (Dynamic)
06. Floating Platform

Zoom Section: Hydraulic Injector
07. Liquid Pressurizing Device
08. Optical Fiber (for Coral Growth)

Kundi Shu, Ka Chung Lo and Xiufeng Li,
Rhizomic Bridge,
Studio 05, Melbourne School of Design,
University of Melbourne, Australia,
2021

above: Organic waste is transported from the local areas to the compost pool for pulverisation, microbial decomposition, fermentation and centrifugal treatment, and is eventually converted into small molecular organic debris – the marine snow. Optical fibres in the pipes aid the phototaxis of marine micro-organisms, diversifying species in new coral reefs.

right: From a pertopian to a utopian vision: the final stage of the bridge construction.

> We need to invest more time exploring the pertopian approach that allows for the essential negotiation between the technosphere, biosphere, ethnosphere and also the noosphere

The students' proposal involves small pylons that minimise damage to the seabed, process organic waste produced locally and transform it into 'marine snow'. The initial pylon was a thin metal-coated structure with optical fibres that were used to encourage coral growth, fed by the marine snow. As the pylons become stronger and able to carry more weight, they also promote the diversity of marine ecology. The bridge incrementally becomes a liveable bridge benefiting humans and other species. It slows coastal erosion and creates better environmental conditions. This marine structure communicates their version of pertopia but, as often happens, the final images reference utopian forms.

Pertopian Dreams
Utopian visions increasingly rely on the technosphere being realised through deterministic but ill-considered solutions to poorly understood situations (not 'problems'). And if the future survival of humanity requires a fundamental reframing of the techno-noosphere, as Pieter Lemmens has pointed out, we need to trigger our desire to change our set of values and the way to live.[6] But even if we believe, as Mike Monteiro states, that 'the world is on its way to ruin and it's happening by design',[7] this can no longer be achieved through dystopian visions. Neither can we rely on utopian images that tell us that everything will be perfect. Instead, we need to invest more time exploring the pertopian approach discussed here that allows for the essential negotiation between the technosphere, biosphere, ethnosphere and also the noosphere, as described by John Allen in his 'Origins of Human Cultures' (2003).[8] When we replace our utopian proposals with pertopian ones, we will be able to dream about a future where rapid change will come from radical environmental and geopolitical triggers and allow us to create not one, but many dreams, as allowed in the Tower of Babel. ⌀

Notes
1. Sim Van der Ryn and Stuart Cowan, *Ecological Design*, Island Press (Washington DC), 2013, p 25.
2. Michael Neuman, 'The Compact City Fallacy', *Journal of Planning Education and Research*, 25 (1), 2005, p 22.
3. Jonathan Rowson, 'Transforming Behaviour Change: Beyond Nudge and Neuromania', Royal Society of Arts, November 2011, p 26: www.thersa.org/globalassets/pdfs/blogs/rsa-transforming-behaviour-change.pdf.
4. Justyna Karakiewicz, *Promoting Sustainable Living: Sustainability as an Object of Desire*, Routledge (Abingdon), 2015, p 171.
5. Mitch Mignano, 'Harmony of the Spheres': https://synergeticpress.com/blog/uncategorized/harmony-of-the-spheres/
6. Pieter Lemmens, 'Thinking Technology Big Again: Reconsidering the Question of the Transcendental and "Technology with a Capital T" in the Light of the Anthropocene', *Foundations of Science*, 2021, pp 171–87.
7. Mike Monteiro, *Ruined by Design: How Designers Destroyed the World, and What We Can Do to Fix it*, Mule Books (San Francisco, CA), 2019, p 9.
8. John Allen, 'Origins of Human Cultures, Their Subjugation by the Technosphere, the Beginning of an Ethnosphere, and Steps Needed to Complete the Ethnosphere', *Ethics in Science and Environmental Politics*, 3 (1), 2003, pp 7–24.

Text © 2023 John Wiley & Sons Ltd. Images: © pp 22–3 © Shi Percy Pan, Yingna Celina Sun and Jiaao Wayne Wong; p 26 © Justyna Karakiewicz; pp 27–9 © Kundi Shu, Ka Chung Lo and Xiufeng Li

Marcus White and Stephen Glackin

Stephen Glackin,
Population change to levels
of local amenity by postcode,
Sydney,
Australia,
2022

Black areas of the map are naturally advantaged by population increase and higher levels of amenity. Grey areas will need to adjust to lower daytime populations (effectively losing amenity due to reduced demand). Crosshatch areas show the opportunity to reuse population increases to expand amenity, and white areas are further disadvantaged by lower populations with low levels of amenity.

The global pandemic and consequent lockdowns have provoked an evacuation of workplaces and urban centres. For society to continue to function, there has been a massive movement towards home working enabled by Teams and Zoom. This has ramifications on not just our lives but also digital infrastructure, commerce and entertainment, as well as a myriad of other dynamics, all of which has totally reconfigured our lifestyles and health in recent years. **Stephen Glackin**, Senior Research Fellow at the Centre for Urban Transitions at Swinburne University of Technology in Melbourne, and Guest-Editor **Marcus White**, discuss this spatial revolution.

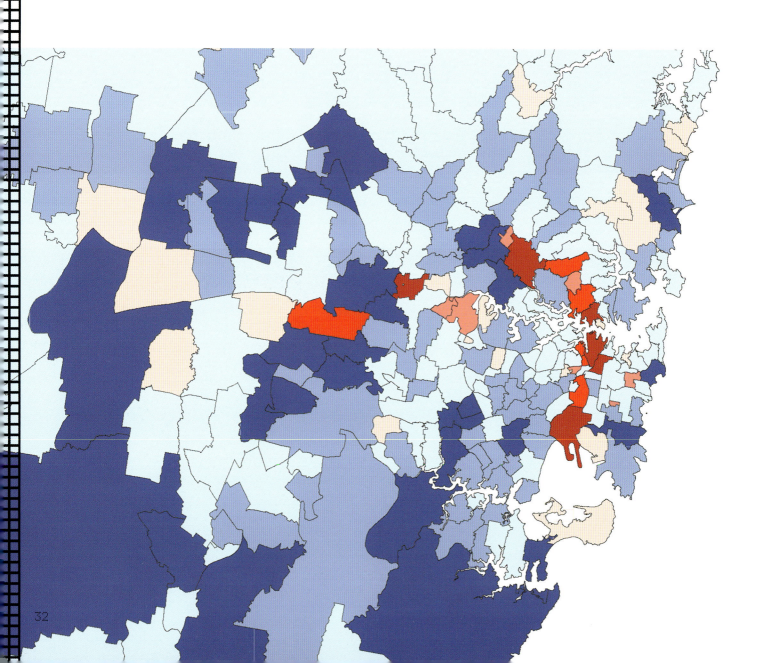

The Covid-19 pandemic has sparked a great rethinking of how we live, where we work and the future of planning, as populations shift to less central locations. In many parts of the world, property prices in the regions around capital cities have jumped significantly in response to the newly established viability and acceptance of teleworking. With many individuals now capable of almost completely working from home, we will see other effects, particularly around the financial feasibility of public transport and central business districts (CBDs), and greater demand for services in the suburbs and other low-density areas, which, until now, lacked the foot traffic to be financially workable.

Now is an opportune time to contemplate the broadband-enabled telework future, the potential positive and negative implications for the urban morphology, and impact on the social and cultural aspects of urbanism. Melbourne architectural practice Harrison and White's Broadband-acre City proposal does this through a re-exploration and reframing of Frank Lloyd Wright's 1932 'Broadacre City' concept. It is time to look at Wright in a new light.

Stephen Glackin,
Daytime population map,
Sydney, Australia,
2022

Daytime population change by postcode in Sydney at maximum work-from-home rates by occupation. Note the additional populations in less central, traditionally lower-amenity areas.

Max daytime population change
- 5,000+
- 2,500 to 5,000
- 0 to 2,500
- -2,500 to 0
- -5,000 to -2,500
- -10,000 to -5,000
- -200,000 to -10,000

A New Freedom for Living?

In recent decades, mass migration and urbanisation have resulted in more than half the world's population now living in cities, with the United Nations predicting that this will reach nearly 70 per cent by 2050.[1] In general, cities are bigger and denser with spaces becoming highly contested and congested. Overcrowding is a growing concern with potentially adverse effects ranging from increased spread of infectious diseases to the impact on mental health. In addition, access to sunlight and public open spaces, particularly green spaces, is becoming increasingly difficult to attain for much of the world's urban population. Clean fresh air is also a critical challenge for cities, with high densities of vehicular traffic and heavy industry leading to heightened levels of noxious gasses and particulate matter increasing the likelihood of respiratory disease and causing millions of deaths each year.[2]

These challenges are redolent of the perils of overcrowding, pollution and congestion emerging from the industrial city of the 1920s to which Wright's Broadacre City was a response. In his book *The Disappearing City* (1932)[3] and a follow-up exhibition of poster panels and large-scale models in the Rockefeller Center, New York, in 1935, Wright proposed an urban proposition in stark contrast to the city-centric slab-and-tower-dominated proposals from his European modernist counterparts. He presented a lateral spread of rural living where each family would have an acre plot of land from the federal land reserves, where residents would experience clean air, be free of congestion and crowding, have space for lush green open spaces for recreation and to grow their own food, where high density only occurred close to the main railway stations and was surrounded by parks. Architecture was to be responsive to the landscape, determined by the character and topography of the region. His panels titled 'A New Freedom for Living in America' set out the key objectives for the proposal and included a list of 'No's: 'No traffic problem', 'No back-and-forth haul', 'No slum', 'No scum', 'No major or minor axis'.

The Broadacre City concept, much like Ebenezer Howard's Garden City of 1902, was blamed by many for the failings of the 20th-century suburban expansion of cities throughout the world, though it is very likely that Wright rightly predicted the mass exodus from problematic cities and sought to design this retreat in a positive way. Unfortunately, the positive aspects of his proposal were lost in the suburban cul-de-sac translation, and the resulting urbanism, commonly referred to as 'sprawl', was a dystopic nightmare of social isolation and physical inactivity as well as non-communicable disease (such as Type 2 diabetes). Most of the population would commute in their automobiles for hours on congested roadways to work in the crowded and polluted cities they were attempting to flee.

Kongjian Yu/Turenscape,
Wangshan Life at Wuyuan County,
Xunjiansi village,
Jiangxi Province, China,
2018

Broadband-enabled Rural Retreat
The expansion of population movement over the last two years, particularly during lockdowns, has included the mass exodus from cities to previously terminal small rural towns. People sought countryside 'tree change', coastal 'sea change' and small quaint 'mountain towns' with 'humble folks', as explored by social observers Trey Parker and Matt Stone.[4] In China, this exodus took the form of a return to village life, as in ecological urbanist and landscape architect Kongjiang Yu's 'Wangshan Life' alternative to innercity living that aims to revitalise decaying, abandoned rural housing. Though begun in 2018, his concept flourished in 2020 and 2021.

The renovated village buildings with new 'cabins', called 'Wangshan Beehives', do not occupy arable land nor visually disturb the original village or overall landscape. They overlook the edge of the crop-producing field and the ancient forest of Osmanthus (devil wood), demonstrating a prototype for a new kind of contemporary 'country lifestyle'.

The small village of Xunjiansi demonstrates Yu's 'Wangshan Life' concept. The strategy involves revitalising and renewing mostly abandoned ancient rural settlements, and upgrading digital infrastructure and dwelling quality to attract city people back to the countryside.

Harrison and White,
Broadband-acre City,
Katamatite,
Victoria, Australia,
2022

above: The Broadband-acre City concept applied to the rural township of Katamatite, northeast of Shepparton (population 433). The rendering shows the non-hierarchical fibre-linked expansion of the existing settlement across the Murray Valley irrigation area.

below: Rendering showing '¼ acre' to 'full acre' plots with detached houses, mixed landscapes including food-producing 'farmettes', solar-power arrays, private gardens, restored native bushland, and mixed-use mini-tower commercial hubs within walking distance of homes.

Harrison and White's Broadband-acre City sees high-bandwidth internet and telecommuting become the catalyst for a return to lower urban densities and the suburban/village idyl.[5] Broadband is used for work, socialising and initiating procreation activities (Tinder, Grindr, etc), and becomes the space of cultural creation. Without the need for social, economic and cultural agglomeration, cultural-economic activity remains at high levels, accompanied by other benefits. For some time, federal and state authorities in Australia have been exploring how to reactivate rural regions with declining populations. These regional areas already have significant infrastructure and land that does not require complex infill/retrofitting of urban landscapes, making them easier to regenerate than existing high-density built environments, and far cheaper to govern. Abundant land becomes an agriculture and leisure resource for individuals, further reducing the need for travel, transport and rates (as governance costs are lower), and supplementing household food. Bringing a workforce back to regional areas that are crying out for agricultural workers, service workers, teachers and health professionals significantly reinvigorates local economies.

Socioculturally, Broadband-acre City provides a return to nature as an integral aspect of humanity and a deeper engagement with outdoor living, promoting healthier, cleaner lifestyles and home-prepared food. There is a significant reduction in fast food, as reduced population density and healthier eating habits make these enterprises unviable. Lower population densities and less social complexity also lends itself to a decrease in conspicuous consumption as there is no crowd from which to stand out. In terms of mental health, several factors also change. With significantly diminished crowding, reduced ('lost in the crowd') social isolation and a potential reduction in ennui is expected, as individuals become more associated and connected with their local environment.

Diasporic Dystopia

However, as the urban diaspora grows, a thinning out of the CBD and inner urban areas occurs, causing service industries such as restaurants and bars to become unfeasible, and a significant drop in land value. With most Australian populations being urban, it becomes a race to the bottom as property owners face ever-decreasing sales values in the city and ever-increasing rural ones. Those unable to flee the city find themselves in boarded-shut, rapidly deteriorating and ultimately structurally unsound living conditions. Cities revert to the urban slums of 1920s Chicago sociology,[6] but without the overcrowding, as everyone else is now in the Broadband-acre City.

In the rural areas, outdated infrastructure strains under the pressure of growing populations, causing catastrophic failure of power, water delivery and sewerage, and additional road traffic, increased road construction and repair costs. Due to the sparsity of the population, the economics of agglomeration and scale make the retrofitting of these areas so expensive that the new rates and services charges push the existing population out and make the once-cheap rural offering financially unfeasible to the new populations. This issue is compounded by the additional logistical demands placed on product delivery, increasing prices and further dissolving the financial benefits that used to function as a correlate of distance from the CBD.

Population density is the most directly related coefficient to amenity. As population densities in both urban and rural areas begins to thin, we will see a rapid decline in the activity of cultural and community hubs, which are reliant on a walkable population catchment to remain tenable. This thinning-out of cultural and social services means those that remain are forced to serve the most dominant local preference and remove specialist and subculturally aligned ventures. A product of this is a homogeneity of venues. Smaller social groups, being less complex, typically have fewer cultural magnets, meaning they tend towards homogeneity, which results in friction between 'insider' and 'outsider' aspects of community life.[8] This reduction in cultural complexity, combined with the reduction in types of viable destinations, equates to a society where 'normalcy' is the only option, leaving those with alternative sociocultural practices on the fringe or worse.

Dystopian main street, Katamatite, Victoria, Australia, 2019

A main street of sparsely populated broadband-enabled dystopia with poorly maintained, crumbling physical infrastructure – a truck-dominated environment not dissimilar to the landscape depicted in George Miller's Australian film *Mad Max* (1979).

Saigon Market,
Footscray,
Victoria, Australia,
2020

The decayed urban fabric of burnt-out and abandoned buildings of the 'old city', crumbling due to the mass exodus from the inner city to the Broadband-acre city.

Tides of Urbanism

As populations emerge from our lockdowns with a renewed interest in the future and ready to reconsider the possibilities of a post-pandemic world, there is cause to consider a new way of life where there are 'No traffic problems', 'No back-and-forth haul', 'No overcrowding', 'No broadband dropouts', 'No buffering' and perhaps 'No need to get out of bed or wear pants for meetings'. However, lower population density may result in higher infrastructure costs, less heterogeneity in services and businesses, greater travelling distances to those reduced services, and potentially a return to the donut cities, where suburban flight leaves the city centres as slums.

For the Broadband-Acre City to avoid these pitfalls, it will still require physical connection, ideally through efficient high-speed rail, in addition to its digital connection, and deep thought will be required to develop de-densification strategies, such as 'mega-garden-city rewilding' or productive urban 'agri-tech landscapes', for existing cities. Regardless of outcomes, telework as a norm will change populations, with a definite trend towards suburbanisation and regionalisation. However, this may just be one of the tides of urbanism, as individuals variously move both to and from the city based on technological change. ⌂

Notes

1. United Nations Department of Economic and Social Affairs, 'World Urbanization Prospects 2018': https://population.un.org/wup/.
2. Philip Landrigan *et al*, 'The Lancet Commission on Pollution and Health', *The Lancet*, 391 (10137), 9 June 2018, pp 462–512.
3. William Farquhar Payson, *The Disappearing City by Frank Lloyd Wright*, Stratford Press (New York), 1932: www.siteations.com/courses/edgeops2014/readings/wk9/wright_disappearing.pdf.
4. Trey Parker and Matt Stone, *South Park* 'City People', season 25, episode 3, February 2022.
5. Raymond Williams, *The Country and the City*, Oxford University Press (New York), 1975; Ferdinand Tönnies, *Studien zu Gemeinschaft und Gesellschaft*, Springer-Verlag (Heidelberg), 2012.
6. William Foote Whyte, *Street Corner Society: The Social Structure of an Italian Slum*, University of Chicago Press (Chicago, IL), 1947.
8. Norbert Elias and John L Scotson, *The Established and the Outsiders: A Sociological Enquiry into Community Problems*, Vol 32, Sage (London), 1994.

Text © 2023 John Wiley & Sons Ltd. Images: pp 30–3 © Stephen Glackin; p 34 © Kongjian Yu / Turenscape; p 35 © Marcus White / Harrison and White; pp 36–7 © Marcus White

Nano Langenheim and Kongjian Yu

THE MEGA-ECO-GARDEN CITY
STORIES OF REWILDING AND ECODYSTOPIA

Over the years, the concept of the garden city has been widely misinterpreted. So argue **Nano Langenheim**, lecturer in Landscape Architecture at the University of Melbourne, and **Kongjian Yu**, professor and founding dean of the Peking University College of Architecture and Landscape and founder principal designer of Turenscape. They introduce a more refined transdisciplinary approach to the greening and wilding of cities and some of the consequent complex ecological issues that have to be addressed.

Turenscape Landscape Architecture,
Fishtail Park,
Nanchang City, China,
2021

previous spread, top left: The floating garden system was inspired by the ancient concept of farming over marshland, akin to that of the Aztec Chinampas, where artificial islands were created using underwater enclosures of reeds heaped with soil, and the ditches between them acted as drainage.

previous spread, top right: In autumn, the trees display beautiful colours. The tree species in the monsoon-flood-adapted park are able to survive fluctuating water levels. The selection was based on native monsoon-adapted marsh landscapes. Perennial and annual wetland plants are naturalised along the muddy shorelines, and lotus plants and reeds cover the lake surface.

previous spread, bottom right: The coal ash waste on site, left from previous land use, was recycled and mixed with dirt from the fishpond dykes to create the small islands, seen here in summer when the trees are in full foliage.

Beneath drained and tamed urban street networks lie extensively engineered webs of immutable concrete pipes, trenches and channels, designed to protect urban citizens from the consequences of floods. These highly controlled networks that shaped cities and towns were considered a crowning achievement of modern urban design at the end of the 19th century. They are, however, neither designed for nor easily adapted to the faster, flashier, more intense storms of climate change and are often overwhelmed by today's unprecedented downpours. Nor was the devastating impact of these century-old drainage networks on the ecological health of waterways and other natural systems foreseen.[1]

Inspired by Edward Bellamy's utopian novel *Looking Backward* (1888)[2] and Henry George's work *Progress and Poverty* (1879),[3] the urban planner Ebenezer Howard published *To-morrow: a Peaceful Path to Real Reform* (reissued as *Garden Cities of To-morrow*) in 1902,[4] in which he describes a decentralised model of development planned on concentric principles, punctuated and balanced with nature through extensive public 'green belts' of open spaces, public parks and farming land.

Howard's late 19th-century abstract, utopian, concentric circular urban development model is here reimagined and adapted for hyper site-specific conditions, waterways, ecology, wildness and nature. While his Garden City concept is still relevant in today's urban fabric, the definition of 'garden' is shifted away from late 19th-century connotations of tame and tidy, inward-looking, manicured, privately owned and appropriated-from-elsewhere spaces, towards a definition that is more mechanistic and which enables dynamic social, hydrological and ecological systems to survive and thrive. The projects illustrated here explore the potentials of this wilder, eco-utopian garden alongside its possible 'eco-dystopian' pitfalls.

Garden Suburbs and Mega Garden Cities

Howard's Garden City model imagined two scales of self-sufficient urban developments of moderate-density living within accessible belts of green space. Satellite towns of 9,000 acres (3,642 hectares), with a roughly walkable three-and-a-half-kilometre (2-mile) radius, housed 32,000 residents while the slightly larger 12,000-acre (4,856-hectare) central cities, with a 4-kilometre (2.5-mile) radius, housed 58,000 residents. When each town or city reached full population, another town would be developed nearby, its footprint strictly controlled by greenbelts.

Over the ensuing century, both scales of Howard's model would be misinterpreted, delivering dystopian outcomes on a global stage. His model of satellite towns, published just before the birth of motorised transport, played into the rise of the private motor vehicle as the primary mode of transport, serving as a justification for the development of sprawling, unsustainable, impermeably surfaced suburbs in Australia, the US and UK. In these developments, his strictly controlled green-belt boundaries would be compromised, diluted and encroached upon by overscaled housing, asphalt- and concrete-covered landscapes.

At the larger scale, his concept of central garden cities would serve as rhetoric for mass urbanisation projects in China, where the concentric diagram was sent rippling over the top of natural features of the landscape, irrespective of existing villages, waterways, wilderness and topography. In Chengdu City, for example, the walkable 4-kilometre radius outlined by Howard expands fourfold, and the population density of 58,000 expands to 16 million.

What was missing in both the suburban and mass urbanisation interpretations of Howard's Garden City model was integration of the ecological and agrarian planning aspects. His green belts, intended as both productive and social landscapes, were replaced with cosmetically designed ornamental lawns, showy parks, hidden hydrology and ecosystem hostility. These fragmented, decorative, manicured gardens are highly unsustainable controlled horticultural environments rather than wild gardens in the city; they are visual rather than productive, referential, and borrowed rather than integral or natural. They consistently fail to become wild.

Site-specific Garden Cities: Ecotopia Cities

Howard's endlessly repeating, site-agnostic concentric circle illustration was intended as a diagram, not a plan. In a real-world context, proximity to water, a forceful, elemental driver of urban development, vital for human and animal survival, disproportionately increases land value in adjacency, resulting in urban development patterns that are bounded by its path through the landscape.

Over the next few decades, through growing recognition of the destructive impact of development, a new concept of utopia began to emerge in literature and planning, championed by the landscape architect and ecolocal planner Ian McHarg in his pioneering 1969 book *Design with Nature*.[5] This 'ecotopian' doctrine advocated an intensely site-specific, ecological modification of Howard's model, adapting it to enhance and enable the continuity of wilder systems, including natural waterways. But these considerations and ecological planning methods impact the shape of Howard's model physically, socially and ecologically. Ecotopia is a far less easy diagram to build than Howard's Garden City.

Nano Langenheim,
Aerial view of Chengdu City,
China,
2022

opposite: The image shows the three inner rings of Chengdu City, the outermost of which is 13 kilometres (8 miles) from the central Tianfu Square. The courses of the Nanhe and Fuhe rivers that originally flowed through the centre of the city are both heavily modified by concrete channels to follow the inner ring road of the city's green belt.

The three projects discussed here aim to bring water into their cores and define new relationships with ecological systems and wilderness to explore the potential of ecotopia. Umbrella City (Arden-Macaulay, Australia) is a design speculation that re-envisions the role of street trees in cities. The Meishe River Corridor and Fishtail Park in China are built projects by Turenscape Landscape Architects that re-envision social and ecological relationships between urban development, stormwater and wildlife.

Umbrella City is located on an urban renewal site 3 kilometres (2 miles) north of Melbourne's Central Business District, on land subject to inundation, bisected by a concrete channelised waterway. Current ambitious projections are that the site will house the population equivalent of one of Howard's satellite towns within the decade. This speculative project re-envisions the street network of the site, adapting its surfaces and structure to prioritise the transfer and detention of flood water. By doing so, the 'garden' of the streets is transformed. Traditional visual roles of street trees, such as delineating pedestrian space from vehicle space and aiding civil identity, are no longer dominant. Instead, street trees become pumps and umbrellas, mechanistic, operational components of the stormwater management system. Instead of popular deciduous European species, dense, fine-foliaged evergreen trees are planted for intercepting rainfall and slowing runoff. Species with extensive, thirsty root systems are required for their constant evapotranspiration rates, to efficiently remove water from detention systems, regardless of season, and in readiness for the next storm. What results is an environmental aesthetic experience. Plantings that enhance streetscape symmetry are replaced by plantings driven by underlying natural conditions and environmental needs.

Unbrella City re-envisions the street network of the site, adapting its surfaces and structure to prioritise the transfer and detention of flood water

Nano Langenheim,
Umbrella City,
Arden-Macaulay,
Melbourne, Australia,
2019

Arden-Macaulay is planted with tree species that assist in stormwater management as the entire street network is reconfigured to detain and transport water. Tree species used change depending on the requirements of the underlying condition. Where trees must clear detention systems, they are selected for their fast transpiration rates; where they are required to intercept rainfall, they are selected for their canopy density.

Turenscape recently undertook the revitalisation and rewilding of the 13-kilometre (8-mile) channelised Meishe River corridor running through South China's rapidly growing coastal tourist city of Haikou, which has a monsoonal climate. The concrete flood walls of the river and piecemeal solutions of riverbed dredging, ornamental gardening and lawn planting were replaced with resilient riparian corridors covered with lush native vegetation; a system of rehabilitated mangrove habitats, wetlands including the 200-acre (81-hectare) Fengxiang Park, and a series of interconnected constructed subsurface flow terraces. The river and its surrounding terrain, the hydrological processes of the waterway, tidal and stormwater flooding, as well as water pollution are treated as a holistic connected ecological infrastructure, a green sponge that both revives and cleans the waterway while integrating recreational and social facilities. The project is a great success. The river water is clean, fish and birds have returned, mangroves are re-established, and the water is again at the city's heart.

Turenscape Landscape Architecture,
Meishe River Corridor,
Haikou, China,
2020

below: Fengxiang Park, with its constructed water-cleansing terraced wetlands. The wetlands can clean 6,000 tonnes of Grade V urban surface runoff daily to Grade III, which is clean enough to swim in, and can purify 3,500 tonnes of domestic village sewage to the same grade after undergoing pre-treatment before being channeled into the wetlands.

bottom: Overview showing Fengxiang Park and its wetlands in the foreground and the revitalised Meishe River, running through the centre of Haikou City, in the background.

In 2021, the practice transformed a 126-acre (51-hectare) former fish farm and coal ash dump in the capital city of Nanchang, Jiangxi Province, within the Yangtze River flood plain in east-central China, with a population of 6.2 million people, into a floating forest that regulates stormwater, provides habitat for wildlife and offers an array of recreational opportunities. Fishtail Park is a monsoon-flood-adapted marsh landscape where tree species are selected to survive fluctuating water levels, and barren muddy shorelines that are often exposed are lushly covered with various wetland plants. The waterfront at the periphery of the park meets the traditional recreational needs of the local population and includes playgrounds and lawns, but also facilitates adapted

ecological recreation such as bird watching, made possible by the park's qualities as a habitat. During 20-year flood events the waterfront zone accommodates stormwater, the boardwalks and platforms are submerged, and the park is temporarily inaccessible to the public. Fishtail Park catalyses urban development and provides a replicable model for the shared challenges that many monsoonal cities in fast-developing regions are facing.

Ecodystopia

However, the concepts underlying ecotopias and ecological planning methodologies, biophilia, bird-friendly cities, cities within forests, flooding-adapted cities and sponge cities, are complex and dynamic. How cities and towns take the best of what Howard's Garden City model had to offer and combine them with these concepts may require acceptance of some hard truths, evolution of the diagram, and changes to lifestyle expectations. Natural systems are messy, they need space, and they may look and operate in vastly different ways to the garden norms to which we have become accustomed.

At times, where development has pushed existing ecosystems to the brink, native animal inhabitants have fought back, sometimes through sophisticated urban-induced genetic or behavioural changes and cultural evolution, sometimes through sheer brute force. All these responses have implications for urban development that aims to be in balance with nature. Urban environments favour only the boldest. Grackles, that have a habit of congregating near artificial light sources, have been known to take over an occasional floodlit parking lot, and omnivorous crows that appreciate the easy availability of food humans provide can sometimes overrun whole cities.

These birds outperform 'shy' urban species and even their less bold rural counterparts, leading to changes and losses in global biodiversity, and may recall images of Alfred Hitchcock's classic film *The Birds* (1963).

Brute force is a less common strategy, but is becoming more frequent. Nordelta, Argentina's best-known gated community, is an example. Built on the wetlands of the Paraná River north of Buenos Aires, its palatial homes and gardens, nestled in a landscape of lakes and streams, were invaded by capybaras which, displaced by the reduction of wetland habitat, destroyed lawns, bit dogs and caused traffic accidents. Similarly, crocodile attacks have increased in recent years in places such as the Philippines, as housing continues to encroach on their habitat. And then there are the well-known urban macaques of Kuala Lumpur which, left starving in the absence of tourists during Covid-19 lockdowns, began thousand-strong gang battles for scraps of food.

In Australia, where native animals and insects can be aggressive if not deadly, venomous snake populations sun themselves on the warm concrete paths of revitalised stormwater treatment parks. Cyclists riding through streets of neighbourhoods that provide foraging for native birds must protect themselves from the sharp, powerful beaks of the native magpies that swoop to attack by covering their bike helmets in spiky cable ties.

But perhaps the most difficult of all to accommodate, particularly when we are discussing the inclusion of water in our cities, is the world's deadliest animal, the mosquito, spreading diseases such as malaria, dengue, yellow fever and Zika. Only with a balanced ecosystem and some human compromise can these ecological planning methods work. Habitats for frogs and dragonflies that eat the mosquito and its larvae are needed, habitats for birds that eat the excess frogs are then also needed, and questions about coexistence – the real, physical spatial requirements required to preserve declining biodiversity and what kinds of wild we value – need to be answered.[6]

Nano Langenheim,
Visualisation of Ecodystopia,
2022

Visualisation of an Australian Ecodystopia in which swooping magpies, venomous eastern brown snakes sunning themselves, and the occasional crocodile must be accommodated and exist in balance with human inhabitants.

Notes
1. Matthew J Burns *et al*, 'Hydrologic Shortcomings of Conventional Urban Stormwater Management and Opportunities for Reform', *Landscape and Urban Planning*, 105 (3), 2012, pp 230–40.
2. Edward Bellamy and Matthew Beaumont, *Looking Backward 2000–1887*, Oxford University Press (Oxford), 2009.
3. Henry George, *Progress and Poverty: An Inquiry into the Cause of Industrial Depressions and of Increase of Want with Increase of Wealth: The Remedy*, AMS Press (New York), 1973. Originally published 1879.
4. Ebenezer Howard, *Garden Cities of To-morrow*, Swan Sonnenschein & Co (London), 1902.
5. Ian L McHarg, *Design with Nature*, Natural History Press (New York), 1969.
6. Henrike Schulte to Bühne, Nathalie Pettorelli and Michael Hoffmann, 'The Policy Consequences of Defining Rewilding', *Ambio: A Journal of Environment and Society*, 51 (1), 2022, pp 93–102.

Text © 2023 John Wiley & Sons Ltd. Images: pp 38–9, 44 © Kongjian Yu/Turenscape; pp 40, 42–3, 45 © Nano Langenheim

Jordi Oliveras

an urban odyssey

city beautiful to city inastagrammable

Zaha Hadid Architects (ZHA), Rublyovo-Arkhangelskoye smart city, Moscow, Russia, 2018

To enhance the form and the relationship between architecture and the city, scalable and parametric geometries are used to give identity and order to the set of buildings, and thus legibility in a morphological space. This break with replicating tradition is strongly attractive nowadays given its originality and the maelstrom of images to which we are subjected.

Professor at the Polytechnic University of Catalonia Jordi Oliveras describes the centuries-long history of 'beautifying the city'. He discusses how utopian ideas of urban form and placement or architectural design can quickly become dystopian by blindly following rules of classical symmetry or ideas of modernist fashion.

The City Beautiful movement was a reform philosophy of North American architecture and urban planning that flourished during the 1890s and 1900s with the intent of introducing beautification and monumental grandeur in cities. Emblematic of this movement was 'The White City', a composition of monumental urban buildings that formed the core of the Chicago World's Fair of 1893. The site's layout was primarily designed by the architects and city planners Daniel H Burnham, John W Root and Charles B Atwood, and the landscape architect Frederick Law Olmsted. It was the prototype of what Burnham and his colleagues thought a city should be: symmetrical, balanced and with splendid buildings. It was also a seminal example of a series of new civic centres that were subsequently built on similar concepts in many American cities – a reformulation and perpetuation of the principles of classical order and monumentality for prominent urban spaces. Just over a century later such great urban ensembles have been replaced by central business districts (CBDs), aggregations of competing tall towers devoid of such classical and aesthetic compositional intentions. Contemporary remnants of the classical, monumental approach to civic design are often associated with totalitarian regimes and other dystopian drivers of urban planning.

```
Daniel Burnham, John Wellborn Root,
Frederick Law Olmsted and Charles B Atwood,
'The White City', Chicago World's Fair,
Chicago, Illinois,
1893
```

The layout of the World's Fair was based on neoclassical principles of symmetry, balance and with splendid buildings. The 'White City' (so nicknamed because of the colour of the façades) had a profound effect on American urban architecture as the origin of the City Beautiful movement and its subsequent achievements.

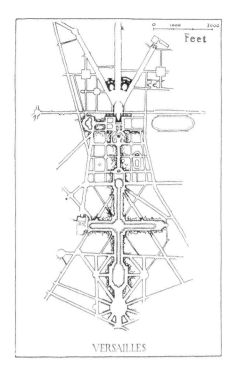 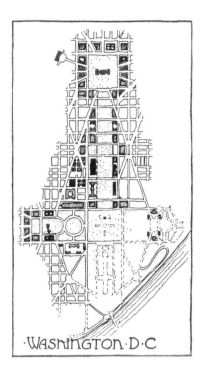 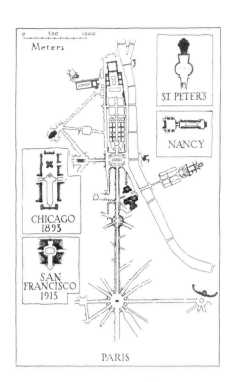

Origin and Heritage of the City Beautiful

The City Beautiful was not utopian in the conventional sense, but can be understood as such. In response to the overcrowded slums and tenements that characterised many cities at the time, there was a widespread yearning to improve cities by enhancing their beauty in the hope that this would also promote a harmonious social order. After the Chicago World's Fair these beautification efforts gained social momentum internationally after being publicised and popularised by the work of journalists and their endorsement and promotion by prominent architects. The 1902 McMillan Commission plan for Washington DC, of which the National Mall is the centrepiece, continues to guide the city's development. The Chicago Plan of Daniel H Burnham and Edward H Bennett (1909) reshaped that city's central area. Architectural features such as geometric order, monumental ensembles and neoclassical buildings began to be used in large plans for new capitals worldwide. The Plan for Canberra, by the American architect Walter B Griffin and his wife, architect Marion M Griffin, featured two main symmetrical axes with broad avenues radiating out from central points. Sir Edwin Lutyens and Sir Herbert Baker's plan for Imperial New Delhi (1931) was laid out in the European Renaissance style with vast green spaces and neoclassical architectural elements with accents borrowed from India's Mughal and Buddhist architecture.

The sources of the City Beautiful's urban aesthetics can be traced to the idealised architectural style of the French Renaissance between the 15th and early 17th centuries known as *la grande manière* (the grand manner) that derived from classicism and the Italian High Renaissance (1495–1520).[1] Layouts of the palatial gardens of large châteaux and palaces of the French nobility were transposed to urban plans that featured wide avenues organised in long axes and large, regular open spaces lined with buildings forming hierarchical and symmetrical sets whose façades were composed according to the classical Doric, Ionic and Corinthian orders of architecture.

This tradition was later updated and reformulated according to the Beaux-Arts school of design and the American aesthetic movement lasting from about 1885 to 1925 that combined elements of ancient Greek and Roman architecture with Renaissance ideas to form the theoretical basis of the City Beautiful movement. Werner Hegeman and Elbert Peets' classic work on city planning, *The American Vitruvius: An Architect's Handbook of Civic Art* (1922),[2] formalises the movement's adherence to Vitruvius' principles of *firmitas*, *utilitas* and *venustas* ('strength', 'utility' and 'beauty') and was to serve as an inspiration for subsequent architects.

Figure from Werner Hegemann and Elbert Peets, *The American Vitruvius: An Architect's Handbook of Civic Art*, 1922

Comparison at the same scale of the Washington Plan of 1902, Chicago World's Fair (1893) and San Francisco Civic Centre (1915) with the Versailles Gardens and Paris's *Axe historique* (historical axis), Nancy's Royal (Stanislaas) and La Carrière squares, and St Peter's Square in the Vatican. The City Beautiful's achievements are heirs to *la grande manière* due their disposition and the magnitude; that is, the monumentality of the urban spaces and their buildings.

Dystopia as Motivation for the Ideal Reform

The great early 20th-century urban challenge from which the City Beautiful movement emerged was the uncontrolled, unplanned growth of multicultural cities in which spaces were crowded, unhygienic, disorderly and often lawless. These challenges still exist in the US and in other countries. There is often the temptation to start a new city from scratch, avoiding the accumulated mistakes and attempted reforms of existing urban agglomerations. From the canonical written utopias and their possible realisations, the same scheme always presents itself: first, a critique of the chaotic existing situation, and second, an alternative solution that solves the perceived problems by eliminating the previous conditions. Traffic congestion, excessive density and accumulated disorder are the main reasons for proposing new cities. Examples for such propositions include: the New Administrative Capital (NAC) of Cairo, under construction since 2015; the masterplan for the Federal Capital Complex of Nigeria, Abuja (Beautiful City), by Kenzo Tange Associates (1981); Nur-Sultan, the capital of Kazakhstan, by Kisho Kurokawa Architects & Associates (1998); and Xiaogan (2019), a satellite city of Beijing, called the 'new Shenzhen of the North', which looks to replicate Shenzhen's growth success, but without some of the original's flaws. Consistent attributes of these plans include urban spaces of wide avenues surrounded by high towers, a certain relaxation of the classical rules in tune with an economic pragmatism, and an emphasis on monumentalism associated with power.

Other Embellishments

After 1893, the implementation of neoclassical composition to improve cities became the dominant convention, making the emergence of other design alternatives difficult. Modern urbanism barely managed to dislodge the idea that when improving the urban fabric, beauty is synonymous with the grandeur of the monumental. The plans and achievements of modernity, including those of Le Corbusier and Lucio Costa's layout of Brasília (1957), failed to detach themselves from the classical idea of great axes and symmetries. In the mass balances of the Chandigarh Capitol Complex by Le Corbusier (1951) or in the Empire State Plaza in Albany, New York (1976) with Wallace Harrison as the supervising architect, mirror symmetries were used. In large streets such as Cornelis Lelylaan in the Amsterdam West Plan (1953) and New Arbat Avenue (formerly Kalinin Prospekt) in Moscow (1967), volume alignments were repeated. They are proposals for an urban monumentality with a modern architectural language. Nevertheless, the composition of these and many similar projects hardly competes with the Beaux-Arts tradition.

```
Skidmore, Owings & Merrill (SOM) and Tom Leader Studio (TLS),
Urban design scheme for the Boot Area,
Xiong'an masterplan, China,
2019
```

Envisioned as a model 'city of the future' for China, Xiong'an will accommodate Beijing's non-capital functions. SOM and TLS prioritise ecology and the human experience through several seemingly contradictory urban design principles: an appropriate urban scale, respect for the natural environment and the introduction of green infrastructure, making the heart of a city more diffuse and less identifiable.

Wallace Harrison,
Empire State Plaza,
Albany, New York,
1976

The plaza is an excellent example of modern urban composition as an alternative to the Renaissance aesthetic. The architect Wallace Harrison and Governor Nelson Rockefeller initially conceived the design in-flight aboard the governor's plane. Administration buildings are integrated with the old State Capitol via the great plaza with its reflecting pools, which is located over a busy underground commercial concourse.

Ricardo Bofill Taller de Arquitectura,
Antigone neighbourhood plan,
Montpellier, France,
1999

Given the lack of a defined form, the axis, as the backbone of urban development, provides a sequence of diverse open and civic spaces. A morphologically intelligent scheme, it is easy to read and recognisable by its inhabitants. To express an architecture that pays special attention to public space it was decided to utilise ideas traditionally associated with beauty and harmony.

Similarly, when we observe masterplans for new developments, we can appreciate how certain consecrated ideas, such as road axes, concentric points or symmetrical geometries are maintained. But often utopian ideals of seeking order become translated into dystopias as the reiteration of perfect symmetries reaches the point of abuse. This dysfunction is observed in Albert Speer's plans for Germania (Hitler's proposed name for a rebuilt Berlin), partially realised between 1938 and 1943; in the Centrul Civic district in Bucharest, remodelled under Nicolae Ceauşescu during the 1980s; in the plan of the Antigone neighbourhood in Montpellier, France, by Ricardo Bofill Taller de Arquitectura (1999); and in the axis of the stylised palm tree within a circle that forms Palm Jumeirah, an archipelago of artificial islands in Dubai, United Arab Emirates, drawn-up by the American architectural firm Helman Hurley Charvat Peacock (2005).

It can be said that modern art such as Neoplasticism or Constructivism, seen in Piet Mondrian's paintings of 1917 and *Proun 1 D* (1919) created by El Lissitzky – to mention only the first compositional exercises proposed as alternatives to the classical canon – does not have corresponding examples in urban architectural art. Two of the few notable exceptions attempting to investigate urban space in a modern artistic language are Cornelis Van Eesteren's Neoplasticism in his plans for The Hague in the Netherlands (1926), and Zaha Hadid's Neoconstructivist studies for an unbuilt masterplan for Zollhof Media Park in Düsseldorf (1989).

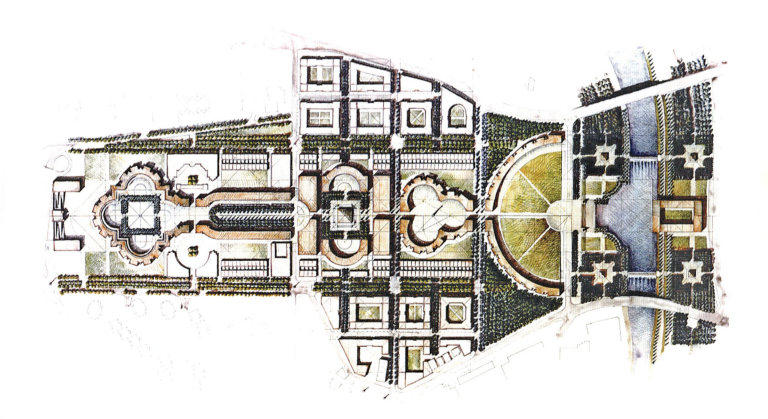

Zaha Hadid Architects (ZHA),
Zollhof Media Park,
Düsseldorf, Germany,
1993

The collage painting for this project is a complex summary where site perspectives, shadow studies and forced views are overlapping on a multiple conjugation of the fragmented series of volumes. The representation technique with transparent layers enhances superposition and juxtaposition as a Deconstructivist aesthetic of sublimation of differences and complexities present in contemporary urban space.

The Beauty of Urban Space

To what extent should the beauty of urban spaces follow an established pattern? To what extent do the most successful achievements of the historical repertoire continue to be a paradigm? What are the renewed meanings of the concept of urban beauty? What urban spaces are cause for admiration, impress us, excite us, or move us? From the monumental axis of the Karnack Temple Complex in Egypt (1500–1200 BC) to that of the Mesoamerican city of Teotihuacán in Mexico (3rd century AD), from Rome's Imperial Forum (54 BC–AD 105) to Gian Lorenzo Bernini's St Peter's Square in the Vatican (1667), from the Gardens of Versailles designed by the landscape architect André Le Nôtre (1687) to the National Mall in Washington DC, envisioned by Pierre Charles L'Enfant in 1791, we find that the interest aroused by these monumental constructions is undeniable because it is sustained by consecrated achievements of other eras. But is the admiration for the monumental and the grandiose still associated with the concept of beauty?

It is difficult to pinpoint the historical moment when architecture began to be considered as the art of publicly displaying power. But we can pose the question as to what, today, is the aesthetic interest of spaces such as Dubai's Sheikh Zayed Road, Doha's Qatar Financial Center or Pudong's skyscrapers in Shanghai? Regardless of their success if measured by the number of times their images have been reproduced, it is notably difficult to find any design principles in these urban fabrics. At the time of the City Beautiful movement, its adherents were convinced that a beautiful environment favours the moral and civil development of its inhabitants. Now we also know that when cities are not only designed to be seen, photographed and communicated, but to be lived in, shared and experienced, this moral and civil development catalyses their inhabitants' identity and social cohesion.

Aesthetics of the Image

Cities are designed so that their implementation is as efficient as possible while satisfying their inhabitants' physical needs, economies and emotions. However, this last aspect, that of aesthetic sensibility, is subordinate to the others, because it is the least quantifiable, the most subjective, and the most susceptible to interpretation and manipulation. The engravings of panoramic views of princely cities and royal palaces were distributed to a wealthy minority, postcards of the World's Fairs were sent by middle-class visitors via postal mail. On the other hand, the online publication and 'likes' of images of unique or interesting public spaces are now disseminated freely through the population via social media.

Today, the aesthetic quality of cities is demonstrated through practicality, and how it is valued by corporations and individuals. This leads one to consider the validity of the very concept of beauty as a consolidated humanist value and to be permanently attentive to new nuances that shape and change it. The concept of urban beauty is experienced by the citizens who reside within these cities or visit them, who enjoy and suffer its benefits and disadvantages. First-hand accounts of their experiences are spread via images in today's world, where the platform of the graphic message is paramount.

The creations of *la grande manière* were conceived from the point of view of the elevated central perspective to visualise the maximum amplitude of a whole. The great views of the princely parks and their layouts were continued in the way spaces of cities were designed everywhere. Let's take, for example, the radial plan of Karlsruhe (1715) conceived in the time of Margrave Karl of Baden-Durlach, almost without distinction between buildings and gardens. Or the geometrical layout linking the Palace area with the new town of Aranjuez (1750), by Santiago Bonavia. Or the harmonisation of squares, buildings and gardens in Nancy (1753) by the architect Emmanuel Héré. Or, also, the garden streets surrounding the palace of Ludwigslust, according to plans by Johann Joachim Busch (1776). We might suppose that the best way to enjoy these urban spaces was at the pace of a horse-drawn carriage.

The Chicago World's Fair, with its 'lagoon', fountains, staircases, porticoes, colonnades and domes, impressed the visitor. These attributes were promoted through photographs on postcards in which the elevated central perspective, foreshortened from the terraces, was suggested.

From the middle of the last century, viewing cities while in motion became the norm both for movie-goers and drivers. The route of the great urban axes as seen from a convertible was the urban spectacle par excellence and led to the popular double-decker tourist bus in large cities.

In the modern era, aerial vision became a consideration. Kasimir Malevich's suprematist drawings, called 'planits', El Lissitzky's geometrical exercises called 'Prouns', which developed volumes into space, and later the avant-garde photographs of Alexander Rodchenko and László Moholy-Nagy, opened a field of artistic vision that city designers would assimilate into their works. Later the fusion of static and cinematic vision formed by a sum of sequences became a common practice. By the end of the 20th century the prestigious skyline profiles that highlighted a city's tall buildings were complemented by the moving camera.

Today, when aerial images of cities have become commonplace, we are getting used to satellite views. In addition to an aesthetic of Kantian contemplation we have passed to the subjective experience that boosts different visions, such as the luminosities of digital and 3D screens and billboards in the manner of Tokyo's Shibuya Station area or New York's Times Square that flood us with visual stimuli.

The Future Civic Art

For real-estate developers and government administrations with decision-making power, development with an eye to the financial statement predominates. The yearning for a beautiful city has often turned into a mere race for dense agglomeration with more surface area in tall buildings. While the best-designed residences remain hidden from the public gaze behind impenetrable fences, corporations situate their headquarters in accessible and effective places lacking representation or meaning. The contribution of architecture to the corporate or governmental image has been to the detriment of other media such as publicity or websites that are reserved for more meticulous design instead of urban environments and building façades.

Recent urban studies frequently analyse dystopian places while avoiding aesthetic considerations. On the other hand, critical rereading of ideal proposals that update the complex concept of beauty are comparatively scarce. In the meantime, 'likes' to instagrammers' posts might give an indication of what is popularly accepted aesthetically. Nevertheless, I am afraid that from these observers and consumers no alternatives to the existing 'Civic Art' can be created or deduced directly. It remains for expert designers to wrestle with the diverse aesthetics of the city. ᗪ

Notes
1. Spiro Kostof, *The City Shaped: Urban Patterns and Meanings Through History*, Thames & Hudson (London), 1999
2. Werner Hegemann and Elbert Peets, *The American Vitruvius: An Architect's Handbook of Civic Art*, Architectural Book Publishing Co (New York), 1922.

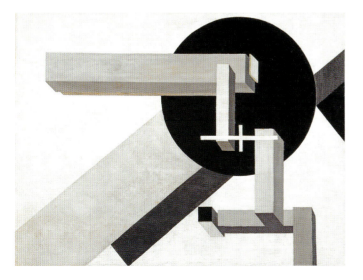

El Lissitzky, *Proun 1 D*, 1919

Prouns (an acronym for the Russian phrase 'project for the affirmation of the new') were a station between painting and architecture. They were milestones in the search for new spatial ideas with the help of axonometric geometry. Some Prouns received nicknames like Town, Square or Bridge, showing direct application to urban design.

Text © 2023 John Wiley & Sons Ltd. Images: pp 46–7 © Zaha Hadid Architects; p 50 © SOM; p 51(t) Photo Jer21999; p 51(b) © Ricardo Bofill Taller Arquitectura; p 52 © Zaha Hadid Foundation; p 53 © Bridgeman Images

Jane Burry and Mehrnoush Latifi

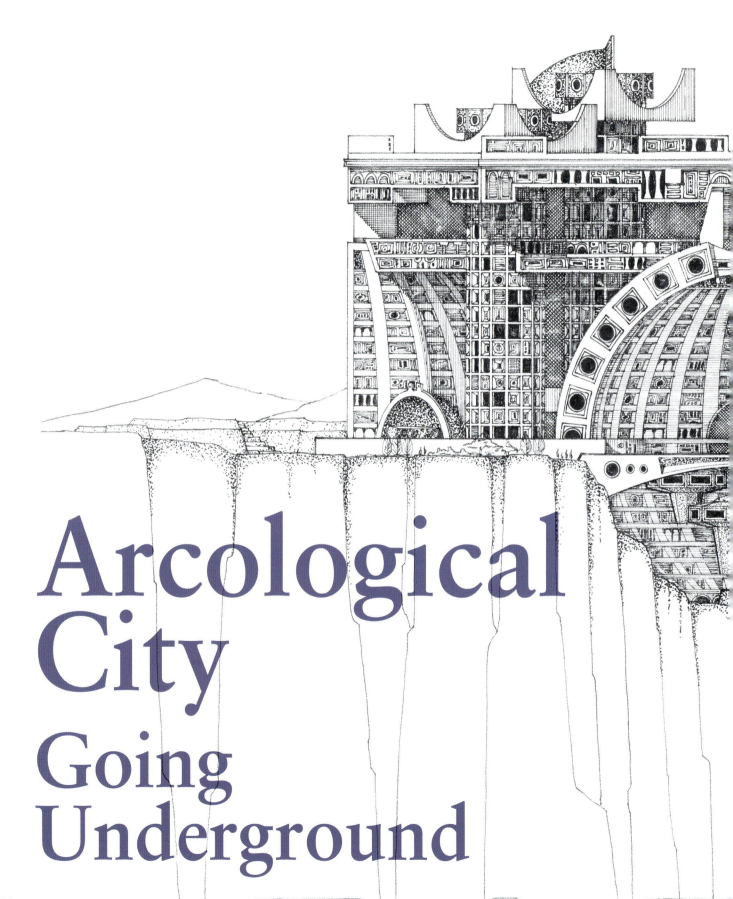

Arcological City
Going Underground

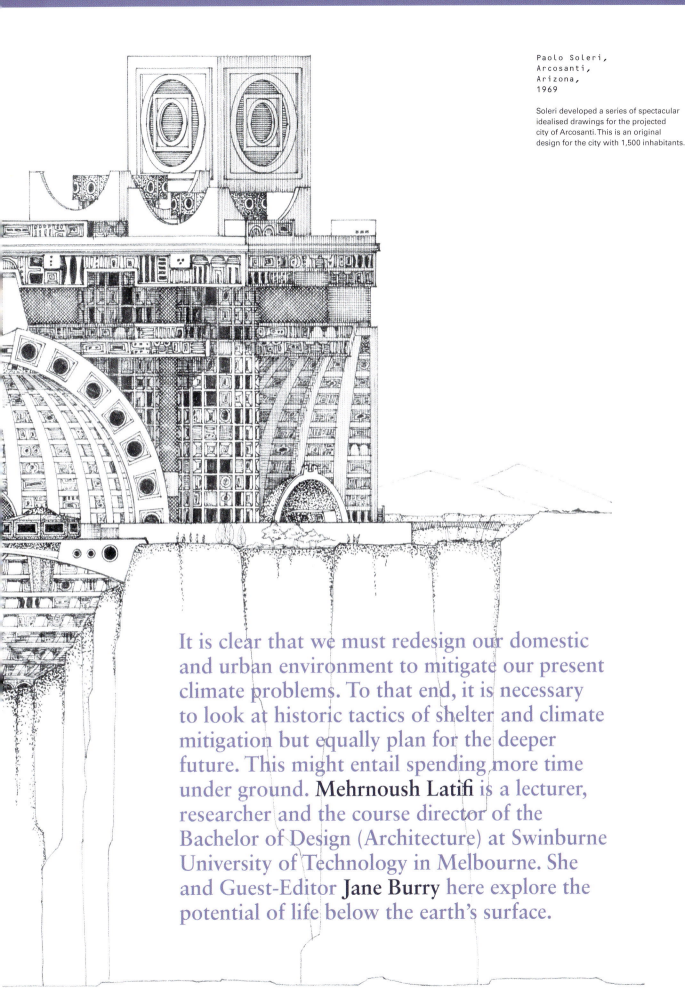

Paolo Soleri,
Arcosanti,
Arizona,
1969

Soleri developed a series of spectacular idealised drawings for the projected city of Arcosanti. This is an original design for the city with 1,500 inhabitants.

It is clear that we must redesign our domestic and urban environment to mitigate our present climate problems. To that end, it is necessary to look at historic tactics of shelter and climate mitigation but equally plan for the deeper future. This might entail spending more time under ground. **Mehrnoush Latifi** is a lecturer, researcher and the course director of the Bachelor of Design (Architecture) at Swinburne University of Technology in Melbourne. She and Guest-Editor **Jane Burry** here explore the potential of life below the earth's surface.

Following decades of climate denial, the world has entered an era when climate change is proceeding at a rate that is tangible, alarming, and unpredictable at local levels. Human systems that threaten climate stability and the manifestations of life on the planet need to be re-engineered and rolled back to slow or arrest change (mitigation) while we plan for the now essential and inevitable need to adapt to the worst effects in the short, medium and longer term. We need simultaneously to change the future that has been forecast, and to shelter from it.

Temperature extremes are one of the major killers in the world today. Infants, elderly people, those with underlying health conditions and the poor are disproportionately vulnerable. The World Health Organization (WHO) recommends living areas be maintained at below 32°C (89.6°F) by day, and 24°C (75°F) degrees by night[1] – indoor temperatures that are potentially costly, energy consumptive and polluting to maintain and sustain during ever-lengthening heat waves. Paradoxically, mechanical cooling also feeds the vicious cycle of exhaust heat from pumps and fan motors that contributes to increasing heat-island effects or concentrations of trapped heat in urbanised areas, exacerbating the problem. Extreme storm events are also rising in frequency and intensity, especially in cyclone- and tornado-prone areas. Records are being broken for high wind speeds, which, given the logarithmic wind-speed profile of the boundary layer, militates against building high above the ground in such areas. Disturbingly, in contrast to the steady rise in average global temperature, some parts of the world have also been experiencing much more extreme cold winters through the changed global patterns. In the US, death rates rise by 8 to 12 per cent in the winter months, attributed to a combination of cold and the related prevalence of colds and flu it brings.[2] Exceptional cold snaps cause spikes in deaths.

Whilst they attend to the urgent mitigation of human impact on the climate by reducing the consumption of energy, resources and carbon emissions, cities across diverse global locations need future ways of protecting their populations and essential services from the increasing extremes of heat, wind and cold. In other words, more passive means are needed to moderate and modulate the internal microclimates of our architecture, optimising it for human health and wellbeing. Where better to achieve this suppression of extremes than within the earth itself?

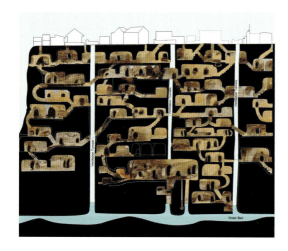

Historical Precedents

When Turin-born American architect Paolo Soleri began building Cosanti, his gallery and studio near Scottsdale in the Arizona desert, in the 1950s, and subsequently in 1970 when founding the idealised equitable and environmental city of Arcosanti about 112 kilometres (70 miles) to the north, he adopted an ancient building approach: earth-casting, using the contours of earth as formwork and excavating the space from beneath the structure. Going underground is a time-honoured approach to security and climate retreat.

Inhabiting the earth or using earth building as a defence against both extreme high and low temperatures have a very long history. Perhaps the best-known underground cities are in Nevşehir province, Cappadocia (from Old Persian *Katpatuka*), now part of Anatolia in modern Turkey but formerly part of the First Persian Empire. Underground dwellings in this region were excavated from layers of soft volcanic rock as far back as the Palaeolithic, with extensive underground complexes being built during the 8th and 7th centuries BC. By 1800 BC these expanded to become entire cities like Derinkuyu, home to 20,000 people escaping the hostility of extreme weather and the constant threat of war, with schools, houses, shopping and places of worship all underground.[3] These cities were further developed by early Christians persecuted for their faith during the Byzantine era. Some underground dwellings were still occupied until the 1950s. This troglodyte (from Greek: meaning cave dweller or, literally, 'one who goes in a hole') approach to dwelling and social interaction was, and is, much more widespread than is generally realised.

Dating back to at least AD 800, the shawadan (or shavadan or shavadoon) has been an underground component of vernacular houses in the hot semi-humid climate of Dezful, one of Iran's oldest cities, which reaches temperatures above 50°C (122°F) in summer. Shavadan is a climate-adaptation strategy, using underground spaces for cooling and accessing underground water. It is a subterranean system with different components such as entrances and stairways, corridors and shafts, halls or *shabestan*, and deeper main halls called *sahn* with underground platforms called *kat* around them. Some houses in Dezful are also connected through the shavadan's tunnels, or *tals*, creating connected neighbourhood-like networks under the city.[4] Many examples of microclimatic lessons learned from the partially subterranean shavadan have been adopted in contemporary Iranian domestic architecture, such as A House in Jolfa District, Isfahan, by Logical Process Architects (2021), creating spaces habitable in all seasons.

Derinkuyu, Cappadocia,
Anatolia, Turkey,
8th century BC to 1950s

opposite top, left and right: A cross-section through the rich tapestry of inner spaces of a city that once had 20,000 inhabitants and included homes, schools, shops and places of worship interconnected underground. This is one of the largest of a network of underground settlements excavated in the soft volcanic rock of the region, a refuge from extremes of weather and aggressors.

opposite bottom: Interior view within the network of interlinked, multilevel underground spaces, staircases and passages. First excavated in 1963 and opened to the public in 1969, Derinkuyu is one of up to 36 such underground cities in the region. It extends over 18 levels of up to 85 metres (280 feet) in depth, and has a breathtaking level of sophistication with its great range of differentiated spaces, ventilation system and wells.

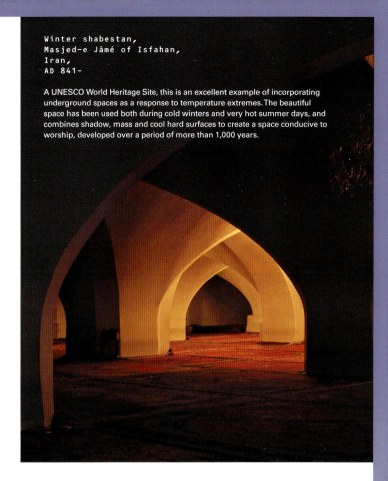

Winter shabestan,
Masjed-e Jāmé of Isfahan,
Iran,
AD 841–

A UNESCO World Heritage Site, this is an excellent example of incorporating underground spaces as a response to temperature extremes. The beautiful space has been used both during cold winters and very hot summer days, and combines shadow, mass and cool hard surfaces to create a space conducive to worship, developed over a period of more than 1,000 years.

Mehrnoush Latifi,
Cross-section through the shavadan of Moeen Tojjar House and connection of houses through *tals*,
2022

The image illustrates the incorporation of shabestan, systems of underground tunnels and halls, into a traditional building to accomplish a temperature differential of 30°C (54°F) between the heat and humidity outside and the cool spaces within.

The Silk Road camel trains, the Berbers in Tunisia and the opal miners of Cooper Pedy in Australia have all escaped from extreme heat and aridity into underground dwellings. Equally, in global cities subject to extreme cold, connected basements form networks of public spaces, such as in the Canadian cities of Winnipeg, Montreal and the capital city, Toronto, which has over 400,000 square metres (5.2 million square feet) of retail space, distributed along 27 kilometres (17 miles) of tunnels connecting 48 office towers, six major hotels and 1,200 stores. City officials estimate that it is used by 200,000 people a day. In other parts of the world, the basements beneath buildings are, at their most prosaic, a resource to increase land use in dense urban areas, even if, as in Australia, this is currently only for car parking. Meanwhile, old mines and military bunkers become data centres and repositories, similarly protected from climate and conflict.

Revisiting Arcosanti

Arcosanti is an experimental town, on 10 hectares (25 acres) of a 1,640-hectare (4,000-acre) land preserve, which – not atypically of such utopian visions – has not been realised in its entirety or at the scale first imagined by its founder.[5] Paolo Soleri worked briefly in 1946 at Taliesin West, Frank Lloyd Wright's winter desert home and architectural laboratory (1937–), but abandoned the master, disillusioned by Broadacre City, Wright's cherished lifelong concept for low-density suburban development. Continuing Soleri's 1968 concept of 'Arcology',[6] which combines architecture and ecology, the non-profit Cosanti Foundation he founded still educates and experiments, open daily to 40,000 visitors per annum. Income from the sale of handmade ceramic and bronze wind-bells, the latter from the town's original foundry, is evidently insufficient to push the population past between 50 and 150 individuals, mainly students and volunteers, just 1 to 3 per cent of Soleri's imagined community of 5,000. Arcosanti is no more built completely underground than it has attained its projected population, but when building its early passive solar-oriented structures, concrete was poured over earth mounds and the soil excavated from under the resulting concrete shell once it had set to create vaults. Conceived as a fantastical car-free antidote to urban sprawl, Soleri's drawn visions for Arcosanti soar 25 storeys into the air. His inspiration, however, comes from the earth, including termite mounds and worm colonies as well as coral reefs.

Paolo Soleri,
Macro Cosanti,
early 1960s

Partial view of a scroll drawing, crayon on butcher paper, scroll #030, used as a promotional poster for the Cosanti Foundation. Soleri designed the bowl as a wind-sheltered volume; he believed that in winter the bowl would be a great collector of sun energy, in summer a vast shaded space.

Logical Process Architects,
A House in Jolfa District,
Isfahan, Iran,
2021

Cross-section through a contemporary Iranian courtyard house, creating in-ground spaces in combination with deep shade, vegetation, water and air movement across the interior to create a pleasant summer microclimate. Overall, it engenders a rich variety of climate experiences for the inhabitants throughout the year.

HKP Architects,
Itäkeskus Swimming Hall,
Helsinki, Finland,
1993

An impressive engineering feat, this 11,000-square-metres energy-saving underground complex was excavated from rock in Itäkeskus, a satellite centre 11 kilometres (7 miles) to the northeast of the centre of Helsinki. It houses three pools, diving boards, a jacuzzi, two large waterslides, an invigorating cold-water pool, five regular saunas and one steam sauna, a gym and a fitness centre. Built over two floors, it can accommodate 1,000 people in the recreation centre, or 3,800 in its alternative function as an emergency civic shelter. This is one of the more spectacular of 400 underground facilities in Helsinki linked by 300 kilometres (186 miles) of tunnels.

City Planning Department,
Underground Masterplan of Helsinki,
Finland, 2011

The masterplan shows existing underground tunnels and spaces in grey, and areas designated for future development in dark blue.

Moving from the sunshine of the Arizona desert in a city where time has stood still, one may go underground in earnest for the freezing Finnish winters of contemporary Helsinki. An underground masterplan for its whole municipal area was completed by Helsinki City Planning Department and signed off in 2021. Conceived to shelter the inhabitants from the extremes of the winter climate, it updates previous space requirements and includes only the most important underground projects, leaving others to complete the details while providing the opportunity for future development by coming generations. A prepper bunker allows for the possibility of 'future Russian aggression'. Helsinki's underground building credentials are already sound. The Temppeliaukio Church, designed by architects Timo and Tuomo Suomalainen (1969), excavated from solid rock in the city's Toolo district, and the Itäkeskus Swimming Hall by HKP Architects (1993) – a large recreation centre that can take 1,000 customers on an average day as well as converting into an emergency shelter with space for 3,800 people – show that Helsinkians mean what they plan.[7]

Zero Carbon Farms,
Growing Underground,
London,
2015

below: Zero Carbon Farms (aka Growing Underground) supplies London restaurants and retailers from their underground farm below Clapham Common in London. The photo shows the early days of experimentation in growing crops using 90 per cent less water, much less space and incurring many fewer food miles than equivalent traditional agricultural methods.

bottom: Richard Ballard and Stephen Dring, his partner in this venture, realised that derelict underground spaces would be a cost-effective way of staying within the urban centre. Microgreens, herbs and salad vegetables in hydroponics beds grow rapidly in these optimal conditions and make an equally rapid transition to plates via local restaurants and major retail outlets.

Meanwhile, Singapore has altered property laws so that the government owns basement areas. In London, the company Growing Underground, founded in 2012, has turned a former air-raid shelter under Clapham Common into the site of a hydroponic vegetable farm for the cultivation of crops such as Thai basil, coriander, pea shoots, rocket and mustard leaf, and in 2015 Low Line Lab began growing vegetables in underground tunnels in New York, powered by rooftop solar panels. While the cost of building new projects underground remains prohibitive, adding excavation and drainage to other construction costs, repurposing pre-built and 'found' underground spaces is not, and the ultimate motivator will be the climate stability and long-term energy savings that can be gained. This applies substantially to both earth-sheltered and fully underground builds.

Gil Kenan, *City of Ember*, 2008

Adapted from the children's post-apocalyptic 2003 book by Jean Duprau, this movie for the young graphically portrays the terminal decline of the underground City of Ember, humankind's now-degrading refuge for over 200 years. As the central generator starts to fail, the lost city elders' carefully stored instructions for the end of Ember come to light, but in the hands of children. Here, Lina Mayfleet (played by Saiorse Ronan) crouches in the underground streets of Ember examining the damaged 200-year-old circular map and directions on a circular city access cover.

Dystopian Speculation

The post-apocalyptic normalisation of future underground living has already been extensively explored in fictional worlds such as the films *Fuga Dal Paradiso* (1989),[8] and *City of Ember* (2008),[9] and narrated in documentary detail in *Dark Days* (2000),[10] which explores the real lives of those living permanently in the underground Amtrack railroad tunnels of New York.

A life in which the surface of the earth becomes a forgotten or uninhabitable realm while all necessities including water, filtered air, artificial UV light, nutrition, clothes, products, education and entertainment can be provided underground is likely to induce panic in claustrophobes. However, they might take comfort in the fact that this would be no more than a 10 per cent shift from contemporary lives that on average are already spent at least 90 per cent indoors.

The concept is not entirely far-fetched. Just as developers' plot ratios have embraced mechanical air conditioning and open planning to enable vast building developments to a depth of plan that could not have been imagined or countenanced generations ago, successful underground living could ultimately lead to the creation of whole cities underground in response to the needs of climate shelter, defence and the compelling economics of saving energy and reducing material consumption. Just as the deep-plan corporate building pipes everything in – air, light, scents, worldly sounds and music – why not do the same underground? How would this differ experientially from the airports, shopping centres and large open-plan offices of today's cities? Despite its extreme climate-change predictions, Australia, at least, does not yet appear to have reached this point, based on observations of the upheaval created by lengthy and laborious ongoing tunnelling activities in Melbourne for one new metro line and an under-river freeway link. Helsinki, however, has the perfect bedrock for its underground city, and this may be key.

Perhaps the greater fear factor in this scenario, as the world emerges from the latest pandemic, is the sharing of air in an underground world, accelerating the spread of airborne disease and even toxins in a way that positive air conditioning pressure in quarantine hotels has only begun to hint at. Then there is the question of the spread of fire and smoke, and the loss of oxygen that occurs in above-ground fires, such as the events that have already reached apocalyptic magnitude and ferocity in recent years. Finally, with rapidly and dramatically rising sea levels, the choice of site would need to carefully consider potential for flooding to avoid distressing scenes like those of the captive third-class passengers below decks in the 1997 film *Titanic*.[11]

Notes
1. World Health Organization, 'Heat and Health', 1 June 2018: www.who.int/news-room/fact-sheets/detail/climate-change-heat-and-health.
2. US Environment Protection Agency, 'Climate Change Indicators: Cold-Related Deaths', updated 2 August 2022: www.epa.gov/climate-indicators/climate-change-indicators-cold-related-deaths.
3. Vladimír Nývlt et al, 'The Study of Derinkuyu Underground City in Cappadocia Located in Pyroclastic Rock Materials', *Procedia Engineering*, 161, 2016, pp 2,253–58.
4. Fereshteh Beigli and Ruggero Lenci, 'Underground and Semi Underground Passive Cooling Strategies in Hot Climate of Iran', *Journal of Environmental Science*, 5 (3), 2016, pp 1–12; Hazbei Morteza et al, 'Reduction of Energy Consumption Using Passive Architecture in Hot and Humid Climates', *Tunnelling and Underground Space Technology*, 47, 2015, pp 16–27; Roya Rezaee, Roza Vakilinejad and Mahshid Shahzadeh, 'The "Shavadun" As an Ecological Solution for Architecture in a Hot Climate', *WIT Transactions on Ecology and the Environment*, 120, 2009, pp 303–13.
5. Arcosanti: https://www.arcosanti.org.
6. Paolo Soleri, *Arcology: The City in the Image of Man*, MIT Press (Cambridge, MA), 1969.
7. Stephen Armstrong, 'The Climate Crisis Will Make Entire Cities Uninhabitable: It's Time to Head Underground', *Wired*, 12 November 2019: www.wired.co.uk/article/underground-cities.
8. Ettore Pasculli, *Fuga Dal Paradiso* (1989; Italy, Germany, France: RAI Radiotelevisione Italiana, Artédis), Feature film.
9. Gil Kenan, *City of Ember* (2008; 20th Century Fox Films, US), Feature film.
10. Marc Singer, *Dark Days* (2000; US: The Sundance Channel, Palm Pictures, Columbia Pictures), Documentary.
11. James Cameron, *Titanic* (1997; US, 20th Century Fox and Paramount Pictures), Feature film.

Text © 2023 John Wiley & Sons Ltd. Images: pp 54–5, 58(t) © Cosanti Foundation; pp 56(tl&tr), 57 © Mehrnoush Latifi; p 56(b) Photo Nevit Dilmen. Creative Commons Attribution-Share Alike 3.0 Unported license; p 58(b) © Logical Process Architects; p 59(t) © Arkkitehtitoimisto HKP, photo Jussi Tiainen; p 59(b) © Helsinki City Planning Department, City of Helsinki Media Bank; p 60(t) © Zero Carbon Farms; p 60(b) © Paul Marc Mitchell; p 61 © Playtone/Kobal/Shutterstock

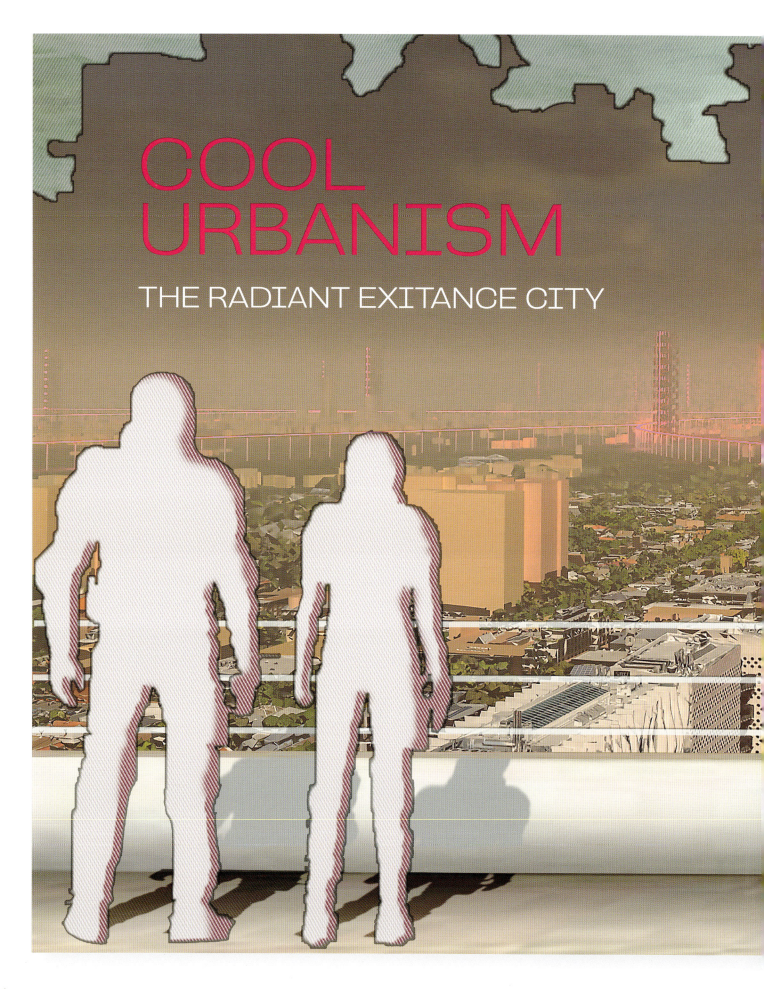

Marcus White/Harrison and White and Tianyi Yang, The Radiant Exitance City, Melbourne, 2022

Perspective eye-height rendering from a terrace showing the expansive view looking across the city of distributed towers in the reimagined version of the Radiant City. The towers nestle into the existing urban fabric while allowing for radiant exitance and particularly longwave radiation urban-heat emittance.

Marcus White and Tianyi Yang

Urban densification is affecting our quality of life – from vitamin D deficiency due to not enough sunlight reaching us in the tall urban canyons that are created by high buildings, to urban heat islands disrupting our sleep, and many other causes of human irritation. Exploring the Radiant City famously proposed by Le Corbusier in 1930, Guest-Editor **Marcus White**, together with Australian architect **Tianyi Yang**, a researcher and lecturer from Swinburne University of Technology and the University of Melbourne, investigate ways to make the model more workable with pencil-thin towers.

Cities are getting bigger, denser and hotter. The impacts of climate change could see temperate, liveable cities become either dryer or wetter, and dramatically hotter in the future.

Using climate modelling and Analogues Explorer from the Australian government's Electricity Sector Climate Information (ESCI) project, it is possible to compare potential future climate or a city's location with the current climate experienced in another location using annual average rainfall and maximum temperature. For example, by 2090, based on Representative Concentration Pathways 8.5 (RCP 8.5), scenarios from those used in the Intergovernmental Panel on Climate Change Fifth Assessment Report (2013),[1] Melbourne's changeable, relatively temperate climate may become like that of other, consistently warmer Australian towns and cities such as Muswellbrook, Scone, Dubbo, Quirindi, Parkes, Forbes, Tamworth, Mudgee, Cowra or Sydney. With this possible atmospheric future in mind, it is necessary to consider the climate-responsive design of cities as they rapidly grow bigger and denser.

Marcus White/Harrison and White and Tianyi Yang,
Climate Analogues Explorer analysis for Melbourne 2090,
The Radiant Exitance City,
2022

Application of Climate Analogues Explorer showing potential future climate with the current climate experienced in another location using annual average rainfall and maximum temperature for Melbourne.

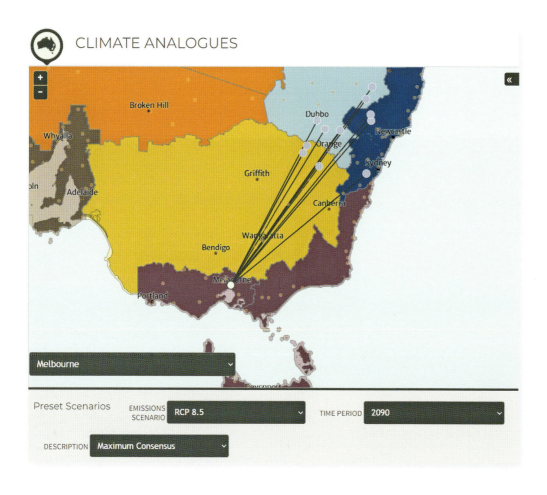

Tianyi Yang and Marcus White,
Sky view factor typological study,
The Radiant Exitance City,
2022

Study matrix showing different densities of urban canyons using the SVF measurement, showing the potential for 'good' urban design (a uniform five-level perimeter block) to trap longwave radiation, thus exacerbating urban heat retention for different urban morphologies. The most successful typology for SVF is found to include a mix of very low buildings with very tall buildings.

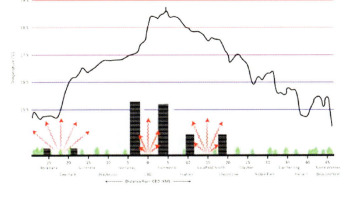

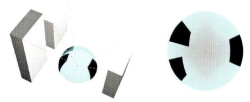

Marcus White and Geoff Kimm,
Urban canyon and sky view factor (SVF) diagram,
2016

The 'trapping' of longwave radiation due to high numbers of urban canyons in high-density urban fabrics, and hemispherical measurement of urban canyons using the SVF metric.

The morphologies of mass urbanisation and densification profoundly impact local atmospheric conditions. The urban heat-island effect, a phenomenon where overnight temperatures over urban centres are considerably higher than the surrounding rural area, speaks of the ways our urban morphologies trap heat. With an expected increase in the frequency, duration and intensity of heatwaves in the future, this lack of overnight recovery and the inability of heat to escape from our cities is a cause of concern for the health of urban citizens. Urban morphologies such as clustered concentrations of towers in central business districts, and uniform zero-setback perimeter blocks of four- to six-level development that have been considered 'good urban design' in the past, must now be questioned. The deep, continuous 'urban canyons' created in these morphologies trap longwave radiation, unwittingly becoming a major contributing factor to urban heat.[2]

The proportion of visible sky above an observation point in an urban canyon is commonly measured as the sky view factor (SVF), a two-dimensional measurement between zero and one. SVF provides an indication of the extent to which urban form allows outgoing longwave radiation (radiant exitance) to be emitted freely to the sky,[3] and is therefore a critical consideration for city designs responding to heat.

Shining Light on the Radiant City

In response to these urban form challenges brought about through climate change and urbanisation, it is worth re-exploring the widely dismissed Ville Radieuse (Radiant City) 'tower-in-park' utopian proposition of Le Corbusier from the 1920s and 1930s. Responding to economic segregation, congestion, overcrowding, poor sanitation, lack of clean air, streets covered in horse manure and poor daylight levels of the 19th-century industrial city, Le Corbusier put forward the 1922 'Contemporary city of three million inhabitants', and explored the concept further in the 1925 Plan Voisin which proposed the demolition of large sections of Paris, documented in *The Radiant City* (1933).[4] The proposed vertical hyper-dense skyscrapers followed a cruciform version of Le Corbusier's Unité d'Habitation, a high-quality mixed-use tower typology with examples built throughout Europe. The best-known of these, built in Marseilles, was known as La Cité Radieuse (1952). This city-scaled proposal achieved high development yield while also providing ample open green space, or 'green lungs'. Though these green lungs were primarily concerned with access to fresh air and visual quality, in a warming climate they would be effective heatsinks providing evapotranspiration through the inclusion of vegetation and also comparatively good SVF ratings, enabling heat to escape the city.

Marcus White/Harrison and White and Tianyi Yang,
Sky view factor analysis of Paris,
The Radiant Exitance City,
2022

opposite: SVF analysis performed on Paris, showing high SVF ratings for the river and main boulevards (red–orange), but low levels within the densely packed traditional street areas of the city (cyan–blue) that have a higher potential to trap heat.

Marcus White/Harrison and White and Tianyi Yang,
Sky view factor (SVF) analysis of
Le Corbusier's 1924 Ville Radieuse,
The Radiant Exitance City,
2022

below: High levels of SVF across the entire city (red–orange) allow longwave radiation to escape to the atmosphere.

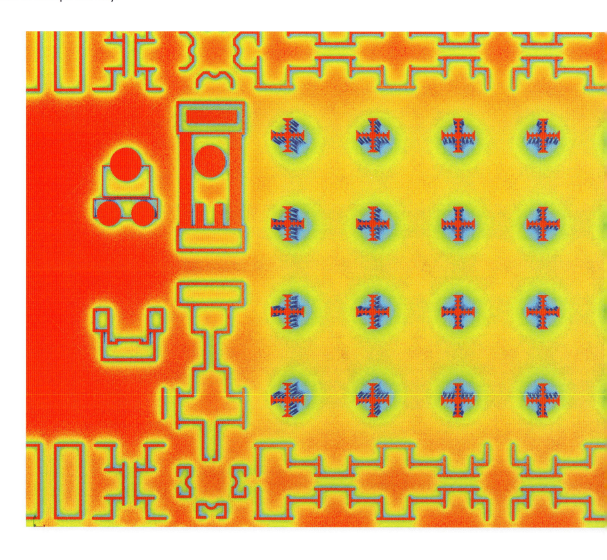

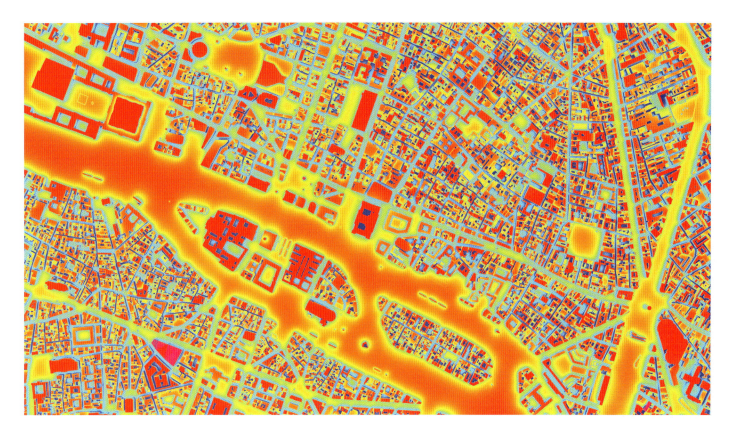

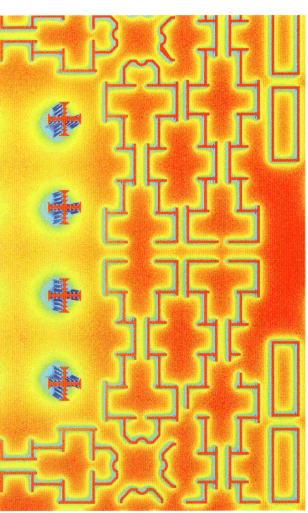

While Le Corbusier's concepts were never implemented on the grand scale of whole cities of towers as he originally conceived, inferior, bastardised versions of his typology were built by others en masse, such as the Pruitt-Igoe social housing project in St Louis, Missouri (1954). Many of these developments mistranslated the surrounding 'park' as surrounding 'car park'; minimised distances between towers and caused poor daylight levels and views; homogenised the intended diverse ownership and mixed-use programmes into housing built purely for the financially disadvantaged, without providing necessary social support; and were built using extremely low-quality construction, no insulation and poor-quality finishes. The urban outcomes resulting from Le Corbusier's mistranslation have been rightly criticised. In 1961 the American-Canadian journalist and activist Jane Jacobs wrote a critique of 1950s oversimplified, 'rationalist' urban planning policies. *The Death and Life of Great American Cities*[5] condemned large-scale modernist development proposals by Le Corbusier and others, and the sentiment has continued to be influential with Jacobs' followers. Moreover, Le Corbusier's automobile-based transport system was way off the mark given what we have learned about the damaging environmental impact of cars. However, the outright dismissal by postmodern 'New Urbanists' and 'Jane Jacobites'[6] misses the unrealised potential of many of the strong ideas he put forward.

Cool Mega-pencil TODs

A slight rethinking of the Radiant City as the 'Radiant Exitance City' may hold many answers for today's urban challenges of densification, urbanisation and urban heat. If, instead of being connected by freeways, the mega-towers were located atop and integrated with rapid-transit nodes (on government-owned land with corresponding air rights in many cases), a kind of extreme transit-oriented development (TOD) could be achieved with substantial reductions in energy consumption and carbon emissions.[7] By prioritising public transport, car-dominated streets could be reconfigured to include increased levels of vegetation. Intensified mixed-income population densities could invigorate surrounding areas that could also support pedestrianised streets and provide diverse retail offerings. In lieu of demolishing areas surrounding the towers, strict redevelopment height limits could be enforced, thus encouraging the retention and improvement of the existing urban fabric. All in all, the impact of these modifications would result in good natural daylight levels and high-quality views for residents of the towers, while keeping the desirable human-scaled old city and its people-friendly urban grain.

By increasing the height and slimming the floor-plate dimensions of the towers to become more pencil-like, the impact of overshadowing would be minimised.

The mix of high but slender towers dispersed through the low-level surrounding development would yield favourable SVF measurements, and thus allow both high population densities and longwave radiation dissipation through the open street canyons for a truly 'cool urbanism'.

Aesthetic alienation associated with densely packed modernist towers is avoided with the megapencil towers distributed atop transit nodes. The towers might be differented through colour, architectural style or form, each perhaps designed by different architects, and could act as visual beacons like church spires, acting as strong urban-transit wayfinding devices to help citizens orient themselves. They could create a beautiful city silhouette reminiscent of the towers of medieval Bologna, with the skyline symbolising the prioritisation of sustainable transport and a climate-responsive city.

Ye Tianyi/College of Civil Engineering
of Chongqing University,
Liziba Station, Chongqing,
Sichuan Province, China,
2004

Liziba Station is an example of extreme transit-oriented development, with a monorail running directly though the sixth to eighth floors of the 19-storey office and residential building.

Marcus White/Harrison and White and Tianyi Yang,
Medieval Bologna full of towers,
The Radiant Exitance City,
2022

above: Digital rendering showing towers spread throughout the low-level urban fabric of the medieval city. While few remain (Asinelli and Garisenda), it is understood that between the 12th and 13th centuries there may have been as many as 180 to 200 towers.

below: Digitally rendered impression of the dramatic skyline of medieval Bologna, with scores of needle-like slender towers of around 100 metres (330 feet) in height punctuating the horizon like a comb with missing teeth.

Marcus White/Harrison and White and Tianyi Yang, The Radiant Exitance City, Melbourne, 2022

Aerial perspective of the speculative reworking of Le Corbusier's Radiant City (1930) showing pencil towers located over railway stations as extreme transit-oriented development, retention of the existing low-density urban grain, reinvigorated pedestrian and cycling infrastructure achieved by closing off selected streets to car traffic, and distributed 'green' heatsinks and parks.

As we head towards a rapidly warming climate, it is imperative that urban designers begin to explore options for city futures that question postmodern notions of 'good' urban design

Not So 'Peachy'?

Of course, the implementation of such a Radiant Exitance City would not be without significant challenges. While re-zoning government-owned land over railway infrastructure might be a cost-effective way of providing 'new land' without the need for mass demolition, stringent height restrictions applicable to other urban or suburban areas would be met with major resistance from existing landowners. There would be pressure to allow high buildings adjacent to the mega-towers, and this would undo all microclimatic benefits of this urban typology. While re-zoning and selling or leasing air rights should provide ample opportunity for legislating mixed private, affordable and social housing within the mega-towers, this process would be susceptible to the kind of powerful lobbying and (alleged) corruption that would potentially result in a perpetuation of housing segregation seen elsewhere. Unless strict, enforceable regulations were implemented for the design and construction of the towers, developers' focus on profit would result in the pencil-like slenderness of the towers giving way to shorter, but much, much deeper floor plates, with poor light levels and air quality, such as exists in the six- to eight-level 'European-style' utopian proposals built during the 2000s along urban transit corridors in Melbourne.[8] Just as in these dystopian, low-slung ghettos, the quality of construction could be extremely poor without stringent oversight, and construction problems would be amplified due to the complexity of such extremely large owner-corporations.

Or, even worse, the towers might retain the height but also 'fatten up' for maximum profit, to resemble those of the fictional Mega-City One featured in the dystopian *Judge Dredd* comic book series by writer John Wagner and artist Carlos Ezquerra. Set in 'New York 2099 AD', Mega-City One is conceived as an answer to the massive overcrowding plaguing the post-nuclear megalopolis of 800 million people. The old city is left to decay under the enormous Mega-Block towers (such as the 'Peach Trees', 'Kidman' and 'Cruise' blocks) housing entire cities' worth of residents living in squalid conditions.[9]

As we head towards a rapidly warming climate, it is imperative that urban designers begin to explore options for city futures that question postmodern notions of 'good' urban design. We must consider a range of design possibilities that can respond to potential climate scenarios such as those extrapolated in the Climate Analogues Explorer. Cities that will be resilient to future climates may not embody the romantic visual unity of old-world European cities; they may be dominated by climate-responsive 300-metre (985-foot) high mega-block towers sitting next to two-storey-high Victorian terrace houses. They may require the Radiant Exitance City for a new kind of 'cool urbanism'. ᐯ

Notes

1. Intergovernmental Panel on Climate Change (IPCC), 'Climate Change 2013: The Physical Science Basis', *Intergovernmental Panel on Climate Change Fifth Assessment Report*, 2013, pp 22, 64, 87: www.ipcc.ch/site/assets/uploads/2018/03/WG1AR5_SummaryVolume_FINAL.pdf.
2. Abdulhamid Ibrahim et al, 'An Assessment of the Impact of Sky View Factor (SVF) on the Micro-Climate of Urban Kano', *Australian Journal of Basic and Applied Science*, 2011, pp 81-85
3. Marcus White et al, 'Cool City Design: Integrating Real-time Urban Canyon Assessment into the Design Process for Chinese and Australian Cities', *Urban Planning*, 1 (3), 2016, pp 25–37.
4. Le Corbusier, *The Radiant City: Elements of a Doctrine of Urbanism to be Used as the Basis of our Machine-Age Civilization*, Faber and Faber (London), 1967; first published in 1933.
5. Jane Jacobs, *The Death and Life of the Great American Cities*, Random House, New York (1961).
6. Marcus White and Nano Langenheim, *The Death of Urbanism: Transitions Through Five Stages of Grief*, AARD Spurbuchverlag (Bamberg), 2020, p 20.
7. Peter Newman and Jeff Kenworthy, 'Urban Passenger Transport Energy Consumption and Carbon Dioxide Emissions: A Global Review and Assessment of Some Reduction Strategies', in Robin Hickman et al (eds), *Handbook on Transport and Development*, Edward Elgar Publishing (Northampton, MA), 2015, pp 36–58.
8. Rob Adams. 'Transforming Australian Cities for a More Financially Viable and Sustainable Future: Transportation and Urban Design', *Australian Economic Review*, 42 (2), 2009; pp 209–16.
9. Alex Garland, John Wagner Block, 'Judge Dredd Wiki': https://judgedredd.fandom.com/wiki/Block.

Text © 2023 John Wiley & Sons Ltd. Images: pp 62–4, 65(t), 66–7, 69–71 © Marcus White / Harrison and White and Tianyi Yang; p 65(b) © Marcus White and Geoff Kim; p 68 © Ruihua Lin

Ian Woodcock

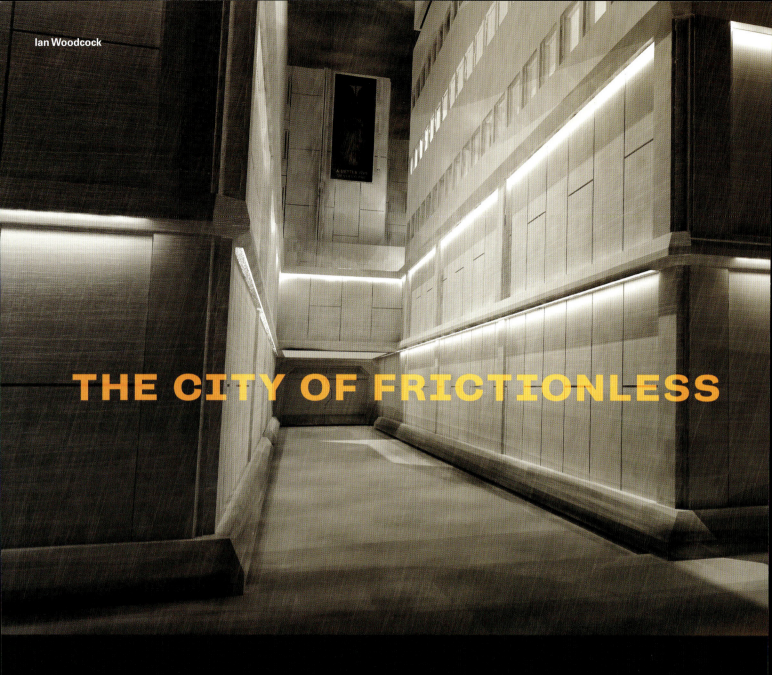

THE CITY OF FRICTIONLESS

'Frictionless mobility', such as through driverless vehicles, has of course been a goal for a very long time in the minds of engineers and designers. But what type of contemporary city might evolve from this? And what happens to other, perhaps more sustainable modes of transport in its wake? **Ian Woodcock**, Senior Lecturer in Urbanism at the School of Architecture, Design and Planning at the University of Sydney, and Adjunct Associate Professor at the Centre for Design Innovation, Swinburne University of Technology, Melbourne, explores these questions and speculates about the city of the future.

MOBILITY

Architecture's utopianism has left a rich legacy of buildings, precincts and districts, manifest in well-known and celebrated approximations of their ideals in places like Paris's Pompidou, London's Lloyd's and the Barbican, Barcelona's Eixample and Amsterdam South. These fragments of varying scales become islands of lofty idealism sitting within broader, more pragmatic and utilitarian urban territories. However, there is one utopian idea that has driven the development of cities for the last century with far more comprehensive effects – the city of frictionless mobility.

This utopia's trajectory has long been highly contested. The dystopia of car-dependent sprawl that billions inhabit is the shocking reality that has resulted from pursuing one approach to eliminating friction at the expense of others.

Michael Mack,
Singulacity,
'Up or Down' MArch design research studio,
Melbourne School of Design,
University of Melbourne, Australia,
2017

With the successful implementation of autonomous vehicles (AVs) within Melbourne in 2040–50, the streets have evolved to reflect new building typologies of warehouse storage and fulfilment centres. Without the need for shops and street frontage, AV-segregated one-way roads are more space efficient, providing optimal circulation routes throughout the city. Studio leader: Gideon Aschwanden.

Paradoxically, many continue to assume that the solution must still be more of the same, only with cleaner fuel and robot drivers, citing the 'convenience' that robot cars will offer without considering the damage this way of thinking has caused so far. However, if the much-heralded driverless cities of the future are not to be even more dystopic autopias than we have so far created, other modes of transport must be prioritised first.[1] In short, driverless cars will need the space freed up by active and public transport to be able to deliver the benefits their advocates have so breathlessly promoted. Recent research at design schools in Melbourne, supports this view.

Frictionless Urbanism: Congestion is Dead, Long Live Congestion!
Central to all good urbanism is ease of mobility that enables accessibility to as much as possible for as many as possible. Friction can be anything that interferes with mobility experience: sharing space with others, trip planning, finding parking, paying tolls or fares, navigating stations, interchanges, transfers and enduring delays caused by intersections, disruptions, accidents and traffic congestion, exposure to inclement weather and more.

In the early 21st century, frictionless mobility is promoted as simpler access to, and coordination between, increasingly diverse transport services via Mobility as a Service (MaaS) platforms. Slick video clips depict urbanites seamlessly moving between work, shopping, entertainment and home, transported by different mechanical devices – e-scooters, e-bikes, metros and driverless taxis – all at the touch of a handheld device for trip planning, booking and payment, for procuring transport and everything else from groceries to venue tickets. Central here is paid access for temporary use, rather than shared occupancy or ownership.

However, the focus on the elimination of friction from travel experience has a much longer history. The need to focus on service integration and safe, secure data flows is largely a legacy of car-dependent urbanism. A century of attempts to eliminate friction from the experience of being in a car, including the act of driving it, at the expense of other modes of travel, has bequeathed massive fragmentation and impoverishment of public and active transport ecosystems that now need reintegrating and expanding. The extended sprawl of contemporary cities means most inhabitants are far more exposed to autopianism than other ways of achieving friction-free travel, and the spatiality of car dependency imposes frictions that are difficult to overcome. In this context, the solution advocated to achieve future frictionless cities is driverless cars (aka autonomous vehicles, or AVs) – an idea that has been around since theatrical and industrial designer Norman Bel Geddes' 'Futurama' exhibit at the 1939 New York World's Fair. While autonomous cars remain only a promise rather than a reality, most of the industrialised world has since been transformed by car-based transport. This continues with ever-increasing road building hyped on the promise of frictionless mobility framed by the big lie of congestion-busting. It has been known since (at least) 1930 that expanding road capacity generates 'induced demand' because, as all good designers know, making something more convenient, safe, attractive, pleasurable, desirable, cheaper or useful will encourage more people to use it, more often. Driverless mobility promises further removal of friction from travel so that we will all be free to go wherever we like, whenever we wish, safely, in comfort without even the friction of having to drive.

Modelling Driverless Autopias
What kinds of cities could evolve on the way to this driverless, frictionless utopia? Those in the business of promoting driverless cars have emphasised the potential for enlarged and more vibrant public realms with more urbane uses, such as retail, entertainment and housing developments on the land currently taken up by on-street parking, and even roads themselves. But modelling of the impact on travel behaviour and land use from driverless vehicles[2] indicates outcomes largely dependent on input assumptions, leaving much room to doubt road space requirements would be reduced or behavioural changes any more beneficial than those related to car-based urbanism so far.

In some scenarios, despite much smaller car fleets, total vehicle use increases dramatically, compounded by circulating empty vehicles. In any scenario with a high proportion of driverless vehicles, while on-street parking is reduced, pick-up and drop-off requirements radically increase to enable continuously circulating vehicles to maximise utilisation, accompanied by greater costs of maintenance and fleet management. If working, sleeping and other activities while travelling become popular, the pressure for ex-urban sprawl and further dispersal and fragmentation of urban land uses would intensify.

In those parts of cities left with any urbanity, serious questions remain around the ability of driverless cars to mix safely with pedestrians, cyclists and other vehicles in complex urban settings. Some have suggested that roadways would need full segregation – for everyone else's safety as much as the flow of driverless cars. 'Futurama' foresaw these issues and proposed entire districts of fully grade-separated central city streets. With a few built examples of actual pedestrian-vehicle segregation, nobody today would dream of offering such an image for public appraisal. And yet, the dream of the city of frictionless automobility persists.

Designing Frictionless Autopias
In 2017, graduate design research studios at the University of Melbourne's School of Design explored future urbanisms that could result from high levels of driverless car implementation. The Singulacity project from the 'Up or Down' MArch studio explored the idea that during the decade 2040–50, monopolisation of urban governance by AI-enabled logistics corporations would overcome community opposition and implement a mass transition to driverless mobility, accelerating the already well-advanced

redistribution of urban production and consumption of goods and services wrought by on-demand supply chains. The focus on warehousing and fulfilment centres via completely virtual transactions enhanced by full automation evacuates all life from the public realm, even in high-density precincts, reducing streets to spaces for driverless movement free of urban interfaces of exchange.

The interdisciplinary MArch and MUrban Planning 'Studio AV: Networks and Space' looked in detail at the precinct- and building-level implications of a shift from bus to driverless taxi access to stations across Melbourne's suburban rail network.[3] This research question was posed by the state transport authority whose high bus subsidies raise the possibility of shifting to taxis. Also, this modal switch is a core assumption in most modelling: cross-town taxi rides are less efficient than taxis for accessing good metro services, and utilisation could be higher than current bus and car access combined due to the induced demand. Students were carefully directed to analyse the actual space required for pick-up and drop-off by different modes of transport historically and according to predictions: airport taxi ranks offered the nearest real-world correlate for driverless taxi transfers and are more space efficient than textbook standards.

Norman Bel Geddes,
Futurama 'Carry-Go-Round',
New York World's Fair,
1939

A precursor to the ubiquitous 'fly-through' of today, visitors experienced the Futurama exhibit as if from an aeroplane, with the god-like perspective of urban planners, accompanied by soundtracks playing through their chairbacks telling them what to look at.

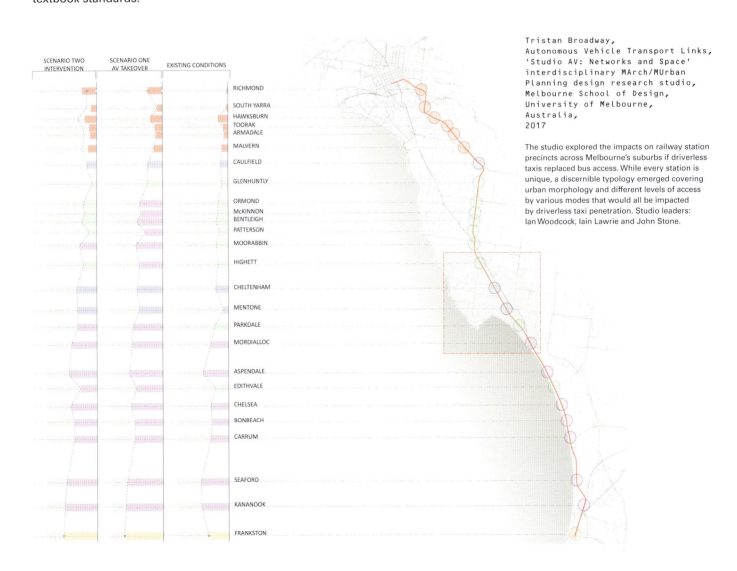

Tristan Broadway,
Autonomous Vehicle Transport Links,
'Studio AV: Networks and Space'
interdisciplinary MArch/MUrban
Planning design research studio,
Melbourne School of Design,
University of Melbourne,
Australia,
2017

The studio explored the impacts on railway station precincts across Melbourne's suburbs if driverless taxis replaced bus access. While every station is unique, a discernible typology emerged covering urban morphology and different levels of access by various modes that would all be impacted by driverless taxi penetration. Studio leaders: Ian Woodcock, Iain Lawrie and John Stone.

Giulia Virgato,
Distribution,
'Studio AV: Networks and Space'
interdisciplinary MArch/MUrban
Planning design research studio,
Melbourne School of Design,
University of Melbourne,
Australia,
2017

right: The replacement by driverless taxis of bus access to suburban railway stations would produce a redistribution of access along the rail corridor; not only would robotaxis increase demand for rail services, but many more stations would become busy transfer nodes, with precincts developing over time to cater to ever larger demand for pick-up and drop-off. Studio leaders: Ian Woodcock, Iain Lawrie and John Stone.

middle: Essendon Station, Melbourne: case study of suburban railway station precinct development over time to cater to increasing demand for robotaxi pick-up and drop off that completely obviates any other kind of development occurring around the station.

bottom: Craigieburn Line corridor: case study showing how land use around the station changes with increased demand for robotaxi circulation and passenger transfer facilities, eventually requiring decking over the railway line.

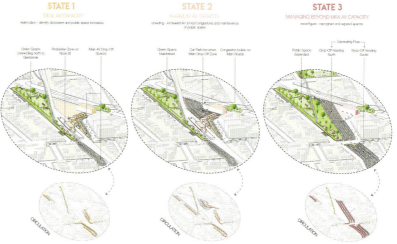

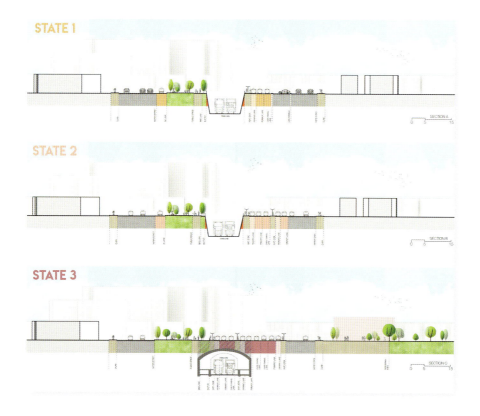

Setting aside serious questions about the capacity to cope of existing road networks serving stations, providing sufficient space for robot taxi pick-ups and drop offs by reassigning the majority of on-street parking spaces and redeveloping station parking obviated all of the benefits promoted by driverless-city advocates. Furthermore, once fixed-route bus services are removed, driverless taxis would encourage redistribution of taxi access along the rail corridors to a wider range of stations to optimise journey times, adding significantly extended pick-up and drop-off zones at many more stations, negatively impacting far more neighbourhoods. It was found that these negative spatial impacts could only be minimised if all driverless taxis were operated as shared-occupancy services, a model that has so far not proved popular for small, low-occupancy vehicles in industrialised societies.

```
Melissa Shao Wei Woon, Jessica Lupita
and Sandra Mansilla Hsyu,
Twenty for Twenty: 20 Minute Neighbourhoods
for 20 Types of Suburbs,
'Zoomburbia 2.0! Future Homes and the
City of Short Distances' MArchUD design
research studio,
Swinburne School of Design and Architecture,
Melbourne, Australia,
2020
```

below: Testing foot traffic. New approaches to planning for retrofitting car-dependent suburbia for local living in '20-minute neighbourhoods' used parametric tools such as Urbano to test scenarios for land-use distributions as walking generators of
new mixed-use/hybrid building types. Studio leader: Ian Woodcock.

The City of Short (Frictionless) Distances

In 2020, the 'Zoomburbia 2.0! Future Homes and the City of Short Distances' graduate studio in architecture and urban design at Melbourne's Swinburne University of Technology explored an alternative response to reducing friction by re-localisation and reducing the need for extended travel. In many cities, travel-time-based urban policies are emerging to focus attention on non-car-based 'friction-free' access to employment, education, services, commerce, recreation and entertainment. Only about 15 per cent of Greater Melbourne (a city of 5 million) meets the criteria for these '20-minute neighbourhoods', so the transition pathways are open for speculation. Much depends on future demographics and how the projected population doubling by 2060 is accommodated. If all future growth were to be focused in the places where non-car-based liveability is already achievable (which is not the same as a transit-oriented development policy), then 65 per cent of the future population could be living locally oriented frictionless lifestyles without substantial change elsewhere. At the other end of the spectrum, as many neighbourhoods as possible across the metropolitan area would find ways to transition to maximise local accessibility. This seems more likely, given the deep cultural value given to neighbourhood character in formal policy and local politics. If so, massive investments would need to be made in creating, implementing and operating the kind of public transport networks needed to provide access from a myriad '20-minute neighbourhoods' to those urban functions that cannot be localised, like universities, major cultural or recreational venues and long-distance transport hubs.

In line with the above, students envisioned streets for the burgeoning diversity of sustainable transport options by subdividing the ground plane for different modes: walking, micromobility (scooters, bikes), road-based mass transit (buses, light rail) and driverless cars. In some ways, this bears a remarkable similarity to the channelised freeways of 'Futurama', but with friction removed for all transport modes. Much of this might appear to have been prompted by the challenge of driverless cars and micromobility, but this is not so new either. Battles to reallocate public space away from cars towards other modes that use space more efficiently, sociably, safely and with less environmental impact have raged in varying degrees around the globe since the advent of motorised travel. To paraphrase a popular quote about the future attributed to speculative fiction writer William Gibson, we can observe the past is still with us, it is just unevenly remembered, and this particularly applies to urban mobility.[4]

Urbanism is well-known for complexity and contradiction. For driverless cars to work as frictionlessly as their advocates envision, paths must be cleared for them to operate optimally, but what kind of city will be worth living in? The space required can be created in two ways: by removing all other modes from their path or by planning for increased use of space-efficient active and public transport. The question is, which path will be most friction-free to get to the city of frictionless mobility? ⌀

Notes
1. Ian Woodcock, Iain Lawrie and John Stone, 'Will Driverless Cars Produce Walkable Cities for Australia?', State of Australian Cities National Conference, Perth, Western Australia, 30 November–5 December 2019: https://apo.org.au/node/306671.
2. Aggelos Soteropoulos, Martin Berger and Francesco Ciari, 'Impacts of Automated Vehicles on Travel Behaviour and Land Use: An International Review of Modelling Studies', *Transport Reviews*, 39 (1), 2019, pp 29–49.
3. Iain Lawrie, John Stone and Ian Woodcock, 'Assessing the Spatial Implications of Autonomous Vehicles as Feeders to Railway Stations in Suburban Melbourne', *Urban Policy and Research*, 38 (4), 2020, pp 357–68.
4. See Quote Investigator: https://quoteinvestigator.com/2012/01/24/future-has-arrived/.

Melissa Shao Wei Woon, Jessica Lupita and Sandra Mansilla Hsyu,
Twenty for Twenty: 20 Minute Neighbourhoods for 20 Types of Suburbs,
'Zoomburbia 2.0! Future Homes and the City of Short Distances' MArchUD design research studio,
Swinburne School of Design and Architecture, Melbourne, Australia,
2020

above: Precinct proposal for transforming the Melbourne suburb of Parkdale into a '20-minute neighbourhood' by optimising for walkable access the placement of new suburban land-use distributions focused on hybridising living, working, education, recreation and health.

opposite: New public urban realms created by reallocating public space in suburban arterial roads to allow frictionless mobility for walking, cycling and public transport, enabling more people to move more easily and safely with far fewer vehicles.

Text © 2023 John Wiley & Sons Ltd. Images: pp 72–3 © Michael Mack; p 75(t) © Bettmann / Getty Images; p 75(b) © Tristan Broadway; p 76 © Giulia Virgato; p 77-9 © Melissa Shao Wei Woon, Jessica Lupita and Sandra Mansilla Hsyu

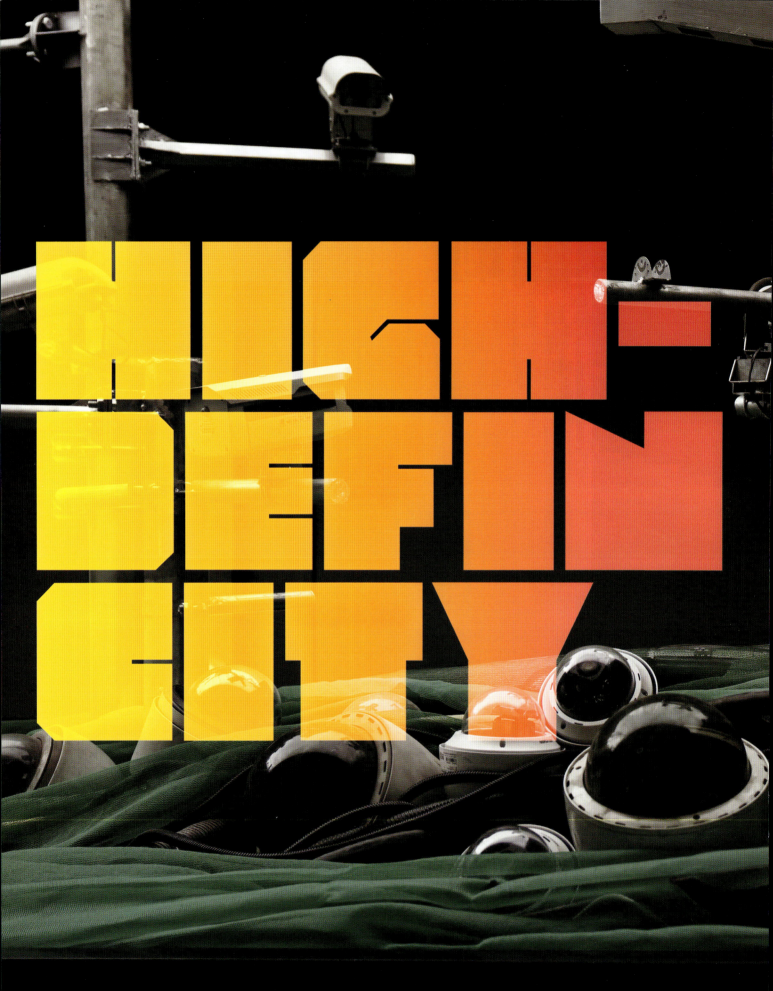

Andong Lu, Jane Burry and Marcus White

ITION
AN INVISIBLE HORIZON OF TECHNOLOGICAL HUMAN SPACE

Guest-Editors **Jane Burry and Marcus White** team up with **Andong Lu**, Lead Professor in Urban Design and Vice-Dean of the School of Architecture and Urban Planning at Nanjing University, to explore the ups and downs of our contemporary condition relative to the exponential rise in the seamlessness of technology – particularly digital technology. This is a complex arena that is both liberating yet can also be invasive to our privacy and dignity, presenting a paradox that they here attempt to unravel for us.

'Perception' has become the technical symbol of the 'humanism' of modernism. In the real sense, individuals are cared for by targeted design through body perception. Modernist designers focus on the flow of time created by motion perception. The body performing in space obtains a non-representative and direct-presence experience through instantaneous perceptual feedback. This sense of presence (a psychological state that arises in situations where no belief suspension is needed), as pointed out by digital media theorist Marie Laure Ryan, is based on mobility and an interactive potential (the original meaning of virtuality). The dynamic experience through space and the physical interaction with things jointly produce a sense of presence.[1]

At the same time, perception accuracy has become a basic human condition due to the rapid evolution of technologies such as augmented reality, biosensors, wearable devices and geolocated cameras. It is hard to imagine going back to a world of low precision – the iteration of old versions of HD video or smoother video games. High-precision perception supported by technology and even defined by it is the basic condition for future human survival. It allows increasing precision in cognition, action and communication, and a unique sense of dynamism, sensitivity and exclusivity. It promotes changes in people's ideas, needs and values, and then profoundly changes design from the user side.

```
PILLS Studio (Zigeng Wang),
Artificial Nature: The Other Fruits,
Baoan district,
Shenzhen, China,
2019
```

previous spread: This piece by Zigeng Wang, founder of PILLS Studio in Beijing and Associate Professor of architecture at the city's Central Academy of Fine Arts (CAFA), focuses on contemporary spatial culture through practice and research. In an old warehouse, a data jungle made of surveillance cameras, electricity poles and construction dustproof nets was created, based on the typical CCTV infrastructure of the city. This jungle is a labyrinth of nerves and blood vessels, where steel generates steel, plastic generates plastic, and fibre generates fibre. This bizarre fertility does not come from the barren soil of electronic waste, but from the images captured by the cameras. People as data feeding the fruit of the forest. People come to this forest and devote a part of themselves to it, and in this way the forest becomes fertile.

```
Andong Lu,
Augmented Human poster for the
project Dwelling in the Mirror,
'Manifestos on Interiority' exhibition,
Nextmixing Gallery,
Shanghai, China,
April 2019
```

right: If Renaissance architecture was based upon a symbolic conception of 'universal human', and modernist architecture on a scientific conception of 'generic human' that conforms to the common rules of mankind, then contemporary technological and humanistic conditions enable us to face individuals with a precision that we have never had before. In this sense, we may once again stand at a new starting point of humanism – the 'augmented human'.

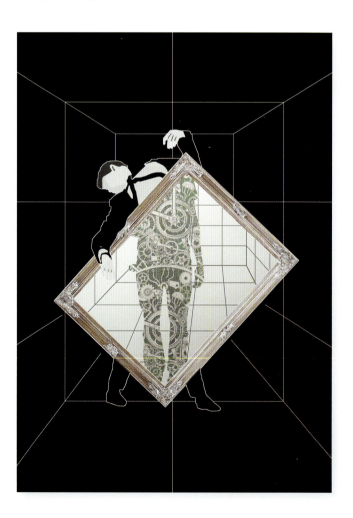

It also brings with it petabytes of shared, high-resolution information and an ever-increasing comfort with or acceptance of not only the sense of one's own presence in a cyber-physical continuum, but with sharing that continuous presence in the world with an unknown cast of others. The Covid-19 pandemic increased the urgency of tracking the presence, movement or confinement of people all over the world. There were QR Code check-ins in Australia and New Zealand, the StopCovid App and TousAntiCovid in France, the Corona-Warn-App based on privacy-preserving contact tracing (PEPP-IT) in Germany, and the 'Hayat Eve Sığar' ('Life Fits into Home') mobile contact-tracing app in Turkey. In China, the Ministry of Information Industry Technology established a nationwide telecom data-analysis platform, collecting data from carriers China Mobile, China Unicom and China Telecom, tracking records of phone users' locations in the past 15 days or up to 30 days. Apps in different regions included dynamic certification of health status of the residents coded as red, yellow or green to impose different levels of restrictions or regulations.

Increasing citizen health and safety through urban planning that includes open and green spaces with access to clean air, and controlled movement and visibility, are ideas that date back to 19th-century interventions such as those of the sanitary movement (1830-40s), Ildefons Cerdà's Teoría General de la Urbanización (General Theory of Urbanisation) (1867) and Baron von Haussmann's boulevards in Paris (1852–70). But this new high-perception environment is polysemic, and new concepts are therefore needed to describe it, and the new role of 'design' within it discovered.

This polysemic space has three parallel and mutually reinforcing dimensions. Firstly, the natural-artificial – the physical environment created by nature and artificially shaped. Secondly, the perceptual-interactive, recognised as created by human perception and the interactions between humans and the physical environment, which takes human perception motor function as its core. And thirdly, the information-content dimension, independent of the physical environment but recognised as the indicative information provided by it. Virtual environments can be regarded as projections of the information-content dimension that can immerse the virtual body as the information medium.

The superposition of these three dimensions in cities constitutes an augmented environment. We often unconsciously experience these multiple dimensions simultaneously, though at any given time or place any one of them might dominate. In these polysemic cities, the innovation requirements of contemporary design can hardly be contained as only pertaining to the formal, first natural-artificial dimension. From the perspective of augmenting the environment, contemporary design must work between all three of these dimensions, and seamlessly intersect with the coinciding dimensions of a myriad of other disciplines.

Francois Penz, Andong Lu and Yiqiao Sun,
Stills from *Back to Balance: An Observation of Post-Pandemic Public Space*,
Cinematic Architecture Workshop,
Nanjing University,
Nanjing, China,
2021

This short documentary film focused on the pandemic's impact on public space in four dimensions: movement, boundary, distance and infrastructure. Students worked in groups to document places they believed had been significantly changed by the pandemic, exploring the intensified levels of observation and cataloguing of human activity and interactions that has occurred. Their instructors then combined their short film montages into a documentary.

Utopia – Eyes on the Street

Jane Jacobs' seminal work *The Death and Life of Great American Cities* (1961) argued for the combination of the first two parallel dimensions of the polysemy environment, the natural-artificial and perceptual-interactive – literally for resident 'eyes on the street' as a natural form of guardianship to prevent street crime.[2] The more people looking out onto the street, the safer it was. Following on from Jacobs' popular phrase was the birth of Crime Prevention Through Environmental Design (CPTED), a term coined by criminologist C Ray Jeffery in his 1971 book of the same name.[3]

In the 1990s and 2000s, the third parallel dimension of polysemic space, the information-content environment, increasingly started to complement the first two in the name of crime prevention or safety in the physical city. Neighbourly surveillance was complemented by CCTV cameras. If windows and balconies overlooking a public area provide the benefits of 'eyes on the street', then the benefit of having hundreds of CCTV high-definition cameras on every street must be even better?

In addition to CCTV, in 2001 a science of urban visual connectivity called Visibility Graph Analysis (VGA) was developed by the British researcher Alasdair Turner and his colleagues of the Space Syntax Group at University College London (UCL).[4] VGA is based on the architectural theory of space syntax to measure visual connectivity within buildings or urban networks using isovist analysis applied at every point on a grid. This method has been applied in cities around the world, and resulting maps showing areas of poor visual connectivity (lower occlusion values) have been found to have a strong correlation with areas with higher incidences of crime.[5] The approach has been suggested to be part of crime prediction at the city scale, but if applied in a *reductio ad absurdum* manner, could also be used to radically reshape cities by designing out or 'removing' spaces for crime, as proposed in Harrison and White's Panopticon Melbourne Central Business District project (2022), which provocatively 'fills in' the much-loved Melbourne laneways.

Marcus White/Harrison and White, Visibility Graph Analysis of Melbourne Central Business District, 2022

Visual integration and passive surveillance map of Melbourne's CBD showing poor visual connectivity within laneways. Melbourne's laneways, such as Hosier Lane, Centre Place and AC/DC Lane, are a hotbed of criminal activities including loitering by non-local people, and degenerate vandalism by Banksy, Keith Haring, Vincent Fantauzzo and other alleged offenders.

Marcus White/Harrison and White, Visibility Graph Analysis of the Panopticon Melbourne Central Business District, 2022

CBD safety improved by applying Crime Prevention Through Environmental Design (CPTED) principles, filling in the Melbourne laneways to greatly improve visual connectivity or passive surveillance and reduce CCTV camera blindspots.

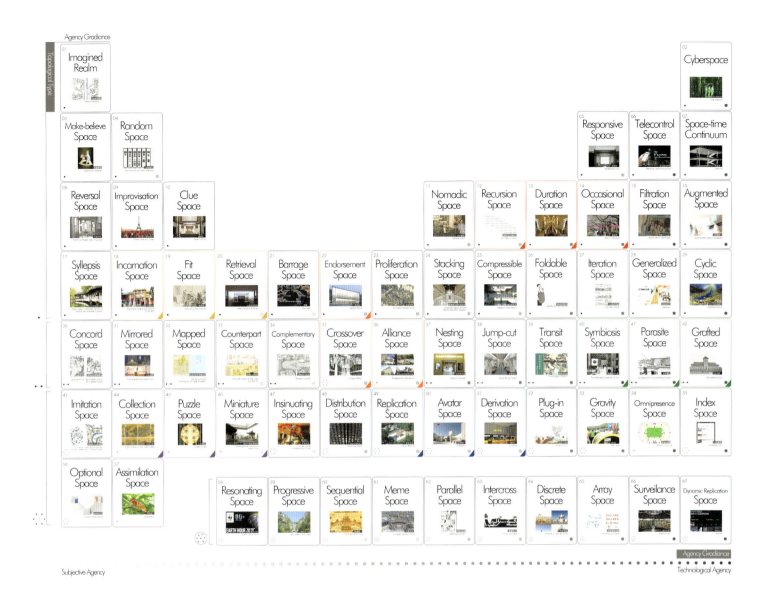

Andong Lu,
Periodic Table of Types
of Spatial Relationships,
2019

We are surrounded by many spatial relationships that do not take or partially take the built form as the carrier. These spatial relationships frame our daily experiences and determine the way we interact with the world. The table here lists 67 types of spatial relationships acting as spatial agency. Vertical axis: topology type (single, one to one, one-to-many, group). Horizontal axis: the transition from subjective agency to technology agency.

The Best of Polysemy

Technology not only blurs the traditional boundary between public and private, but also releases people from the time and space of specific places. The screen (and the practical application of wearable devices under 5G conditions) will become a connection channel between places in different times and spaces. It is no longer possible for citizens to be in one place at a time; they must exist in many different places at the same time. It is, then, up to citizens to determine how the narrative of their existence in polysemic space is juxtaposed, combined and cut together. People can no longer exist as passive users of places, accepting *a priori* existences in the relationship between man and earth, but must become masters of the relationship *between* places, producing *genius loci* through human field interactions, a 'becoming' in the process of continuous change and creation.

Marcus White/Harrison and White,
HD-Eyes on the Street – Under His Eye,
2022

above: Satirical collage exploring a *reduction ad absurdum* increase of surveillance, melding Jane Jacobs' concept of 'eyes on the street' (1961) and George Orwell's 'Big Brother is watching' from *Nineteen Eighty-Four* (1949) with Margaret Atwood's *The Handmaid's Tale* (1985) in which a heavily armed guard is placed on every street while undercover police ('Eyes') are spread through communities.

Andong Lu and Jiayue Qiu,
Polysemy as a Technological Human Condition,
Nanjing University,
Nanjing, China,
2020

opposite: Augmented place makes sense only against a techno-spatial continuum. Presented in fragments, the 'interiors' (synthetic worlds) here will produce new connections and orders underpinned by technology. This new condition calls for attention to new forms of spatial organisation and new modes of experience based on embodied interaction.

The Worst of Polysemy

Contemporary technological and humanistic conditions enable places to accurately and delicately exchange content and information and interact with physical and mental subjects. It is worth noting that this technology-augmented place has constituted a universal real daily life in which other actors present are not always seen or sensed. In this new place, 'geographical integrity' is inseparable from the new technological system. For example, within this techno-spatial continuum, the combination of cameras and machine learning can pinpoint individuals – illegal immigrants, for instance – with *Blade Runner*-reminiscent precision.[6] The 'augmented place' is both an emergent reality and the new ground for planning, in which the goals and priorities also shape the experience.

While we have a more inclusive design, just like video and audio in a film, the technological, social and spatial components are never socially or politically neutral.[7] Prioritising surveillance for street-crime prevention, for instance, can create not simply safer but also socially disempowering spaces.[8] It creates a more accurate sense of place through the synthesis of media, but leaves sufficient space for the participation of many eyes and ears. Surrounded by many spatial relationships that do not take or partially take the built form as the carrier, city inhabitants in their roles, whether as guardian neighbours or law enforcers, live in various synthetic worlds and construct meaning and value in them. The continuous sharing of slices of the HD information-content dimension of this life leads to the construction of diverse meanings and values. We are in an era of augmented place, creating both heightened experience and expanded presence. But in this new polysemic virtual, real, multidimensional environment, have we placed insurmountable burdens on the shoulders of design and on individual citizens to narrate and master their own place within it? ∆

Notes
1. Marie-Laure Ryan, *Narrative As Virtual Reality: Immersion and Interactivity in Literature and Electronic Media,* Johns Hopkins University Press (Baltimore, MD), 2001, pp 69–74.
2. Jane Jacobs, *The Death and Life of Great American Cities*, Random House (New York), 1961, p 458.
3. C Ray Jeffery, *Crime Prevention Through Environmental Design*, Sage (Beverly Hills, CA), 1971.
4. Alasdair Turner, 'Depthmap: A Program to Perform Visibility Graph Analysis', *Proceedings of the 3rd International Symposium on Space Syntax*, Vol 31, London, 2001, p 31.
5. Silvio Melo Junior and Robson Canuto, 'Applicability of Isovists and Visibility Graph Analysis for Evaluation of Urban Vulnerability to Crime', in Alessandro Camiz, Ilaria Geddes and Nadia Charalambous (eds), *Cities as Assemblages*, Proceedings of the XXVI International Seminar on Urban Form, Vol 2, Nicosia, Cyprus, 2019, pp 329–40.
6. Ridley Scott (director), Hampton Fancher and David Peoples (screenplay), *Blade Runner* (film based on Philip K Dick's 1986 *Do Androids Dream of Electric Sheep?*), The Ladd Company and Shaw Brothers (Blade Runner Partnership), Warner Bros, 1982.
7. Bent Flyvbjerg and Tim Richardson, 'Planning and Foucault', in Philip Allmendinger and Mark Tewdwr-Jones (eds), *Planning Futures: New Directions for Planning Theory*, Routledge (London and New York), 2002, pp 44–62.
8. Chiara Certomà, 'Expanding the "Dark Side of Planning": Governmentality and Biopolitics in Urban Garden Planning', *Planning Theory*, 14 (1), 2015, pp 23–43.

Text © 2023 John Wiley & Sons Ltd. Images: pp 80–1 © Pills Architects; pp 82, 85–6 © LanD Studio; p 83 © Francois Penz, Andong Lu and Yiqiao Sun; pp 84, 87 © Marcus White / Harrison and White

THE PROMISES OF POSTCOLONIAL UTOPIAS

Perspectives from the Global South

The notion of 'smart cities', with their ubiquitous linked sharing of data and observation, can be both problematic and simultaneously utopian. **Tridib Banerjee**, Professor Emeritus of Public Policy at the University of Southern California (USC) where he previously held the James Irvine Chair in Urban and Regional Planning, explores the recent adoption of the concept, particularly in the Global South. Notably, Le Corbusier's modernist city of Chandigarh in India has just been named a smart city. What will this mean for law and order, culture, and urban vitality for its inhabitants in coming years?

Tridib Banerjee

Marcus White, Aerial view
of Chandigarh,
India,
2022

A recent aerial render capturing Chandigarh's contemporary urban sprawl expanding from the original 23 sectors in the early 1950s to the current 81 sectors. While spreading over different jurisdictions, Le Corbusier's plan still defines the incremental order of the contemporary urban expansion.

Today the concept of the 'smart city' is trendy in the Global South. Its popularity is promoted by promises of automation, sensors and artificial intelligence, and the ever-expanding possibilities of cyberspace. Global capital and corporations, with vested interests in information and communication technology and AI, are responsible for promoting the notion of the smart city. Examples like Songdo (2015) in South Korea, and Masdar (2010–) in Abu Dhabi are meant to demonstrate how future smart cities can be energy efficient, resilient and sustainable. Contemporary urban problems are seen as results of ineffective management that can be improved by sensors, data, and algorithms for processing big data. The smart city movement is driven by several value paradigms: 'seamless efficiency, responsive transparency, empowering devolution, and shared stewardship'.[1]

But can the smart city also be humane, just and inclusive? This question is particularly relevant today, in the context of this active pursuit of the elusive notion of the 'smart city' that nevertheless lacks a specific definition or concrete suggestions as to how it might improve social and public life. Consider the smart cities programme involving 100 cities in India. In 2015, the Indian government launched its Smart Cities Mission (SCM) by inviting cities to offer visions of 'smart solutions' for effective infrastructure, governance, sustainability and public services. The value paradigms noted previously remain at the core of the SCM challenge, while conceding that 'there is no universally accepted definition of a Smart City'.[2]

Smart City: A Technological Utopia?

It can be argued that the contemporary visions of smart cities do not differ from the long tradition of utopian thinking about urban planning and design that has involved ideas, ideals, ideologies and idiosyncrasies through the ages.[3] Although architectural utopias carry concrete visions of form, they do not necessarily convey ideas about social life and attendant urbanism. Similarly, social utopias typically lack a concrete vision of urban form. As urban theorist Kevin Lynch noted in his book *A Theory of Good City Form* (1981), 'few utopian proposals deal with place and society together'.[4] Particularly in the case of smart cities, this seems to be the case. Occasionally we might see rather sterile renderings of such cities, but a sense of their urbanisms remains absent – invisible and inaudible. Even in the case of the few noteworthy demonstrations of 'smart cities', while these are technologically impressive they can hardly match the culture, urbanism, and the daily celebration of public life and spaces of their traditional urban context.[5]

A more connected world

Flat vibrant vector illustration showing a more connected world using 5G wireless technology in different fields: virtual reality, clean energy, smart city, smart industry using robotics, smart transport, smart farming and smart home. Such utopian images, however, fail to anticipate the potential dystopic social outcomes.

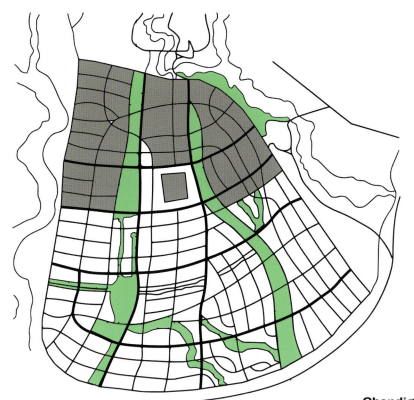

Mehrnoush Latifi, Redrawn and rendered schematic of Albert Mayer's 1949 Plan of Chandigarh, India, 2022

Inspired by the Garden City movement, this plan was informed by the site's natural features, and the variable organisation of residential spaces was defined by the vehicular and pedestrian movement system. Le Corbusier's later plan accepted Albert Mayer's general schema, including the location of the Capitol Complex and the system of open spaces, albeit organised in a more orthogonal and rational order.

Utopias and Dystopias: Between Heaven and Hell

Utopias are places of perfection, where 'perfection is obtained in laws, government, and social conditions',[6] implying a higher level of development. Another meaning more relevant here is the Latin meaning of the word: 'noplace', which is similar to its Greek meaning that combines *ou* (not) and *topos* (place) and that also means 'nonplace'.[7] The notions of 'non-place' or 'placelessness' would be the obvious tropes for postcolonial utopias.

In contrast, images of dystopias or cacotopias – the obverse of utopias – are often more specific and impressive. 'Hell is more impressive than heaven,' observes Lynch.[8] Referring to the classic book *Invisible Cities* (1971), where Italian writer Italo Calvino offers an imagined conversation between Marco Polo and Kublai Khan, the great 13th-century Mongolian ruler of China, about cities around the world, Lynch notes: 'The dialog is a great panorama of utopia and cacotopia, which explores, in a wonderful, circling fantasy, the relations between people and their places.'[9] Drawing from Lynch, then, we may conclude that utopias are always accompanied by their more existential and vivid antithetical realities, or outcomes. This is as true for the smart city imaginaries of today as it is for earlier legacies of postcolonial utopias and even much earlier visions of canonical cities of the Global South.[10]

Chandigarh: A Postcolonial Utopia

After Independence in 1947, India's political leadership wanted a postcolonial urbanism of modernity. The planning of Chandigarh, a provincial capital of the partitioned state of Punjab, offered that opportunity. The utopian ambitions for this new city were shaped by the well-known Gandhi-Nehru dialectic on the future directions for the country. While Nehru desired the urbanity of modern industry and commerce, Gandhi remained committed to community life in the rural tradition which was then the primary habitat for 80 per cent of the Indian population.[11] This tension was captured in the confluence of two utopian traditions popular in the middle of the last century: the Garden City and the Congrès internationaux d'architecture moderne (CIAM) movements, interestingly both growing out of a deep antipathy for the urban heritage of contemporary industrial cities, and their dystopic urbanism of anomie, disease and pollution. Both tried to offer a vision for alternative urbanism of future cities that promoted community and social life, healthy environments, communion with nature, access and mobility for all.

Although famously associated with the plan for Chandigarh, Le Corbusier was not involved in the initial stages of its planning. Albert Mayer, an American planner and a protagonist of the Garden City movement, shared with Nehru his predilection for urban village concepts and the idea of superblocks and neighbourhood units as the basis for organising the spatial order of the city. Mayer's initial plan for Chandigarh (1949) was a fan-shaped layout, comprising residential units of varying size, organised around the site's topography, streams and gorges. To retain the pedestrian culture of Indian cities, the plan separated high-speed vehicular traffic from the pedestrian and bicycle traffic. Schools, parks and other community facilities were distributed within the residential units. The administrative complex was situated at the top of the plan.

It seems Mayer's plan failed to convince the leadership with the images it conveyed. Le Corbusier arrived in 1951, commissioned to deliver a high-modernist vision of the city. Steeped in the rational thinking of CIAM and his own antipathy for the organic medieval urban form, he proceeded to standardise the dimensions of the residential units of the Mayer plan and converted the fan-shaped layout to an orthogonal grid of large superblocks. These superblocks, or sectors, were assigned to different income classes or bureaucratic ranks, reflecting the existing social order of the city. But the informal-sector workers who came to build the city were not included in this scheme. They created their own temporary settlements – *jhuggis* – on the periphery and in the interstices of the planned city, which soon became permanent informal settlements. Considered eyesores, many of them are now consigned to peripheral land or walled enclaves.

Le Corbusier,
Palace of Assembly,
Chandigarh, India,
1962

This monumental architectural landmark is another notable example of brise-soleil architecture attempting to offer an endogenous, utopian vision of modernity.

Le Corbusier,
Secretariat Building,
Chandigarh, India,
1953

A major iconic landmark in the Capitol Complex designed by Le Corbusier. The striking architectural form results from an effort to introduce deep louvres (brise-soleils), overhangs and recessed openings to minimise exposure to the sun and obtain a natural cooling effect.

Albert Mayer and Le Corbusier,
Public open space in Chandigarh,
2004

A view of the current landscape improvements undertaken by the local government of Chandigarh in the dedicated open space preserves along existing streams, as envisioned in Mayer's original plan and subsequently incorporated in Le Corbusier's final design.

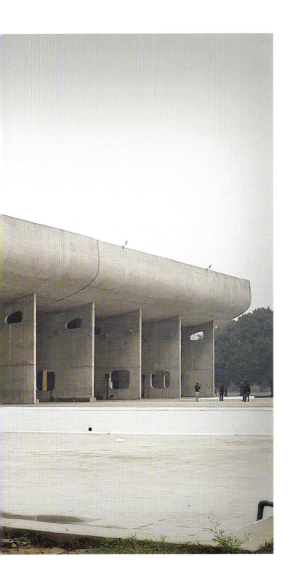

Tempted to connect the plan of Chandigarh to earlier models of canonical cities of China or India, historian Ravi Kalia thought that the placement of the capitol was 'analogous to that of the head in relationship to the body' and that 'Mayer was reaffirming the allegorical reference to the Indian caste structure in the story of Purusha' in the Vastu-Purusha Mandala.[12] Kalia is correct in referring to the social ordering of the caste system specified in this canonical model, as the Chandigarh plan indeed codified a social ecology of ordering by income and rank. The dystopic order of class, exclusion, inequality and separation was institutionalised – if not by Mayer or Le Corbusier, then by the Indian bureaucracy deeply influenced by the legacy of *homo hierarchicus*,[13] reinforced by the colonial order of segregation.

In the more than 70 years since its inception, Chandigarh has gone through major transformations. The urban sprawl of the 'mythical' designer city has expanded from its original 23 sectors to the current 81, while loyally adhering to the original sector dimensions as units of growth. Expanding to the east of the original city, new growth has included an industrial district for information technology. The local government has taken significant measures to bring more foliage and landscaping to the dystopic heat island created by the vast and barren paved concrete spaces of Le Corbusier's Chandigarh Capitol Complex. These improvements may have brought some relief for the lower-echelon workers who had to walk between his architectural masterpieces. Perhaps the most significant achievement of the local government was to transform the open space preserves along existing streams, as intended in the plan, into nicely landscaped public spaces. Chandigarh is now called the 'City of Gardens', memorialising the utopian vision of the Garden City movement. But the city still lacks the sensory stimuli, verve and urbanism of other, more typical Indian cities. The streets are efficient but quiet and sterile.

Nek Chand,
The Rock Garden,
Chandigarh, India,
1957–

What began as a small and hidden garden created by Nek Chand, a road inspector for the local government, is now a major complex of public spaces occupying 70 hectares (175 acres) of land. This project is an exemplar of the bottom-up approach to endogenous city design – a counterpoint to dystopia.

It remains to be seen if these new smart city initiatives will be able to redress the undesirable outcomes of the last 70 years of urban planning and build upon the legacy of the Garden City and CIAM movements, and bottom-up initiatives like Nek Chand's Rock Garden

Another significant modification to Chandigarh is the Rock Garden (1957–), another marvel of landscape design produced locally – indeed secretly in the beginning – by Nek Chand Saini, a local government official. With the urban detritus of broken pottery shards, bangles, bottles and ceramic insulators, Nek Chand designed and built sculptures, murals and public spaces integrated within the natural landscape of the city's streams and gorges. What began as a secret garden occupying 5 hectares (12 acres) has now expanded to a 70-hectare (175-acre) complex of well-designed public space, promoted by the local government.

The original residential architecture of the sectors was designed by the likes of Pierre Jeanneret – Le Corbusier's cousin, later appointed as the city's Chief Architect – and the husband-and-wife team of modernist architects Maxwell Fry and Jane Drew, in collaboration with local Indian architects Aditya Prakash and MN Sharma, with innovative ideas of tropical architecture such as brise-soleils and exposed brick appropriate for the local climate. Chandigarh today is the most prosperous city of India. In the wealthier sectors the tropical architecture is being replaced by tableaux of air-conditioned mega-mansions of hybrid, phantasmagoric 'Indianised' architecture, underscoring the growing dystopia of inequality.

Returning to the Smart City
In 2016 Chandigarh was designated a smart city by the Smart City Commission of the Government of India. According to the website of Chandigarh Smart City Limited,[14] the vision includes infrastructure projects – water supply, sewerage, sanitation and urban transport – with innovative solutions. The idea of e-governance is integral to making the city a vibrant regional centre, but there is no mention of it becoming an inclusive city.

It remains to be seen if these new smart city initiatives will be able to redress the undesirable outcomes of the last 70 years of urban planning and build upon the legacy of the Garden City and CIAM movements, and bottom-up initiatives like Nek Chand's Rock Garden. Or will it simply lead to 'unsmart' outcomes, as Darshini Mahadevia has argued from her study of the smart city initiatives in Ahmedabad?[15] While the initiative's aim has been to transform the informal to formal – that is, 'unsmart' to 'smart' – through infrastructure development, the result has been 'the creation of "unsmart" geographies and "unsmart" conditions for low-income households in Indian cities'.[16] Social exclusion, peripheralisation and marginality seem to be the obvious outcomes of the smart cities initiative.[17]

Today, major street intersections of Chandigarh are fitted with cameras checking for traffic violations, replacing the traffic police. Might this be the beginning of a surveillance regime? Could the mythical city of Chandigarh with its complex legacy succumb to the dystopic outcomes of the smart city movement? ⌂

Notes
1. Dietmar Offenhuber, 'Tarzan vs IBM: Value Paradigms of Urban Technologies', in Tridib Banerjee and Anastasia Loukaitou-Sideris (eds), *The New Companion to Urban Design*, Routledge (London), 2019, p 537.
2. Balaji Parthasarathy and Brinda Sastry, 'Intelligence for Place-Making and Social Inclusion: Critiques and Alternatives to India's Smart Cities Mission', in Banerjee and Loukaitou-Sideris, *op cit*, pp 571–81.
3. Tridib Banerjee, *In the Images of Development: City Design in the Global South*, MIT Press (Cambridge, MA), 2021.
4. Kevin Lynch, *A Theory of Good City Form*, MIT Press (Cambridge, MA), 1981, p 60.
5. Linda Poon, 'Sleepy in Songdo, Korea's Smartest City', CityLab, Bloomberg, 22 June 2018: www.bloomberg.com/news/articles/2018-06-22/songdo-south-korea-s-smartest-city-is-lonely.
6. Merriam-Webster Dictionary, 'Utopia': www.merriam-webster.com/dictionary/utopia.
7. Banerjee, *op cit*, p 197.
8. Lynch, *op cit*, p 69.
9. Lynch, *op cit*, p.72; see also Italo Calvino, *Invisible Cities*, Harcourt Brace Jovanovich (New York), 1974.
10. Banerjee, *op cit*.
11. Sunil Khilnanai, 'India's Theaters of Independence', *Wilson Quarterly*, 21 (4), Autumn 1997, pp 16–45.
12. Ravi Kalia, *Chandigarh*, Oxford University Press (New Delhi), 1999, p 59.
13. Louis Dumont, *Homo Hierarchicus: An Essay on the Caste System*, University of Chicago Press (Chicago, IL), 1970.
14. Chandigarh Smart City, 'About Us': www.chandigarhsmartcity.in/about-us.
15. Darshini Mahadevia, 'Unsmart Outcomes of the Smart City Initiatives: Displacement and Peripheralization in Indian Cities', in Banerjee and Loukaitou-Sideris, *op cit*, pp 310–26.
16. *Ibid*, p 321.
17. Parthasarathy and Sastry, *op cit*.

Surveillance cameras, Chandigarh, 2011

These are now commonplace at many street intersections of the emerging smart city vision of Chandigarh. Is this the beginning of a surveillance regime in urban space, a dystopic outcome for the future city?

Text © 2023 John Wiley & Sons Ltd. Images: pp 88–9, 92(b) © Marcus White; p 90 © DrAfter123 / Getty Images; p 91 © Mehrnoush Latifi; p 92(t) © Deepak Bahl; pp 93–4 © Tridib Banerjee; p 95 Photo Rishabh Mathur. Attribution-ShareAlike 2.0 Generic (CC BY-SA 2.0

Jane Burry

National Security Agency (NSA),
Intelligence Community Comprehensive National
Cybersecurity Initiative Data Center,
Utah,
2014

The centre is atypical for the comprehensive nature of the content matter of the data it is thought to process, but typical of a new non-urban typology: the massive, faceless, secure, all power- and water-consuming data centres found from Utah to the Mesas of Arizona.

ZONING FOR THE LATEST REVOLUTION

CITÉ INDUSTRIELLE 4.0

Although presenting a utopian vision of socialist urbanisation and placemaking, French architect-urbanist Tony Garnier's proposed Cité Industrielle, conceived in the years around 1900, was responding to imperatives that were vastly different from our present-day context. Guest-Editor **Jane Burry** examines its potential as a beneficial predecessor that may have some important lessons for us in our virtual, synthetic, technologically ubiquitous world. Equally she also sounds a 'dystopic alert'. There are always two sides to the urban coin.

Since the plough first displaced people on the land, since the first Industrial Revolution moved the populace from the land to mills, some have benefited and some have paid an unconscionable price. For the working population, the cost of the First Industrial Revolution (c 1760–1840), in terms of lost income, early mortality and quality of life, far outstripped the general benefits, not just for a couple of years, but for a duration of several generations. Artisanal spinners and weavers lost their livelihoods with the development of water- and steam power, and children were the new, economical and size-appropriate workforce in the mechanised workplaces. Large sectors of the adult male population were put out of work.[1] The integration of agriculture and cottage-scale industry gave way to concentrated communities with the factory at the centre. William Blake's 'dark satanic mills' in his poem of 1804[2] demonstrate contemporaneous recognition of the massive social upheaval unfolding at that time.

New urban typologies developed in response to the new industrial order: the mill-town, high-density worker housing in proximity to the factory. Factories were initially located next to natural waterfalls, such as at New Lanark (1786) in Scotland, and later harnessed steam power. The British industrial model spread to other countries in the 19th and early 20th century, and the social lessons and philanthropic approaches to the early neglected needs of worker communities were also adopted and manifest in architecture in some of the new urbanisations. Colònia Güell, founded in 1890 at Santa Coloma de Cervelló, a textile factory town built by Count Eusebi Güell, is one famous example. Güell commissioned Antoni Gaudí to design the Church of the Colònia Güell (1898–1914) and Francesc Berenguer i Mestres and Joan Rubió y Bellver, prominent Catalan *Modernista* architects, to design other significant cultural, agricultural cooperative and residential buildings.

Each industrial revolution introduces a new level of automation to reduce human labour and increase productivity. The Second Industrial Revolution (1870–1914) brought electrification and mass production, and also generated factory typologies and associated worker settlements. Consider the Highland Park Ford Plant in Michigan (1908) by Albert Kahn Associates, the site of the first moving production line, opened in 1910 and coined '90 acres under roof'. Le Corbusier considered Lingotto (1916–23), the Fiat factory in Turin, Italy, by Giacomo Matté-Trucco, with its iconic helical ramp, one of the most impressive sights in industry and, notably, a guideline for town planning.

The Third Industrial Revolution, in the mid-20th century, heralded by nuclear power, electronics, telecommunications, digital computers and growth in biotechnology, was arguably cleaner and marked a shift in employment from secondary to tertiary industries. However, it only slightly impacted the zoning and separation of production from other aspects of urban life that industrialisation introduced.

Fast forward to the Fourth Industrial Revolution (2011–), the silver bullet of the seamless digital pipeline of design and making, the Internet of Things, fully integrated online, digital, virtual, physical and now metaverse. Overall, the 'big-tech', seamless digital economy, greater automation, robotics and artificial intelligence, despite the promise of borderless sharing and distributed resources, seems to be concentrating wealth as never before. How does this manifest in the urban reality of cities, shaping settlement and population in comparison to the revolutions that preceded it?

URBAN UTOPIA: GARNIER'S CITÉ INDUSTRIELLE
Historically, cities have grown in association with substantial agglomerated centres of industrial output. By the mid-20th century, distributed inner-city artisanal workshops and yards integrated with housing areas were substantially displaced to outlying industrial zones of larger-scale manufacturing. There were conflicts between the extensive land footprint needs of increasingly large-scale, often noisy polluting industries with major energy and water demands, and the other social, dwelling, cultural and commercial trading functions of the city. In this matter of urban zoning there is one name that stands out: the French architect and city planner Tony Garnier. His Prix de Rome-facilitated Cité Industrielle project for an ideal city, developed while residing in the Villa Medici in Rome from 1900 to 1904, although hypothetical in nature, modelled on French novelist Émile Zola's socialist utopian *Travail* (1901),[3] was to profoundly influence modernist urban planning in the 20th century. It coloured Garnier's approach to some of his own built public projects in Lyons, but more significantly was taken up by the Congrès internationaux d'architecture moderne (CIAM), from which platform it fundamentally shaped new city planning, such as the relocated Brazilian capital, Brasilia, developed by Lúcio Costa, Oscar Niemeyer and Joaquim Cardozo from 1956. Thus, its underlying ideals about city zoning infiltrated modernist urban planning throughout the world.

> CITÉ INDUSTRIELLE IS SURPRISINGLY FORWARD-LOOKING IN MANY WAYS. LOCATED IN SOUTHEAST FRANCE, ON A PLATEAU BETWEEN HILLS AND A LAKE TO THE NORTH, AND A RIVER AND VALLEY TO THE SOUTH, IT HAS PLENTIFUL HYDROELECTRIC ENERGY GENERATION

Tony Garnier,
Cité Industrielle,
Southeast France,
1904

top: Cité Industrielle is a hypothetical utopian project conceived by Garnier while in Rome, funded by his Prix de Rome for an industrial city to be sited on a plateau in Southeast France. Set out on idealistic lines, it profoundly influenced modernist planning, in particular urban zoning, locating industry away from housing and cultural and commercial areas and in proximity to energy and water.

bottom: Large-scale industrial production as a city driver, architectural and planning inspiration ran deep in this early modernist ideology. This image of a Tony Garnier drawing for Cité Industrielle portrays and celebrates the blast furnaces. The dam for production of hydroelectricity is clearly visible in the background.

Cité Industrielle is surprisingly forward-looking in many ways. Located in Southeast France, on a plateau between hills and a lake to the north, and a river and valley to the south, it has plentiful hydroelectric energy generation. Its factories are located close to a large dam across the valley to generate hydroelectric power and supply water, while its civic area is on the plateau and includes government, museums, exhibition spaces, sports stadia and a theatre. Housing is orientated to take advantage of the sun and wind. All these separate zones are well linked by road and path, to one another and to the agricultural zones. There is a historic quarter close to the railway station, ready for heritage tourism. The 20th-century new towns can immediately be read in this clearly zoned blueprint. However, they did not extend their social utopianism to the extremes of Garnier's idealised future socialist city, which dispensed with the need for a police station, courthouse, prison and even hospitals, with crime and ill-health seen as preventable products of the inequitable system and the poor urban planning and conditions then pertaining.

UTOPIA REVISITED

How does Garnier's vision for a thoughtfully zoned, modernist, socialist settlement answer the needs of the post-pandemic, Industry 4.0 world of the 2020s over a century later? Clearly, his environmental approach remains visionary, with fully renewable energy generation and considered use of passive climate design for housing. But how do his zoning innovations stack up? Whether we are already fully immersed in the era of Industry 4.0 or still sailing towards it, what is known is that it kicked off in Germany at the 2011 Hannover Fair and had become German government strategy by 2013. Its nine pillars – cyber-physical systems, the Internet of Things (IoT), big data, additive manufacturing (3D printing), robotics, simulation, augmented reality, cloud computing and cyber security – encompass the principles of the much greater customisability of products, horizontal integration across whole value-creation networks, and vertical integration throughout manufacturing networks. These networks can include many and diverse nodes including devices such as sensors, and virtually linked feedback mechanisms. In the context of the city, this means, at one end of the scale, the smart factory – 10,000 or more square metres of largely human-free robotic activity. At the other end, miniaturised sites of production of, in some cases, miniaturised products.

When a network exists in cyberspace, the physical nodes and distribution of physical spatial activities acquire new freedoms.

March Studio and Rigmarole,
Abbotsford St,
North Melbourne, Australia,
2022

below: This architectural and design office and workshop, shared by architects March Studio, who build and prototype both here and on site, and furniture and design manufacturing company Rigmarole, is an exception to the rule, thriving in one of the innermost suburbs of the city while all of the immediately surrounding small factory buildings are either already being converted to housing or are on the market.

bottom: Physical modelling and prototyping are fundamental to March Studio's design methodology and innovative architectural output. Some of the furniture design and fabrication is linked to the architectural projects, some commercially independent. The combined studio, digital fabrication workshop, offices and social areas are representative of the new cyber-physical Industry 4.0 design-intensive production linked to culture and art that thrives in the highly networked domain of the inner city but now has only very rare opportunities to do so.

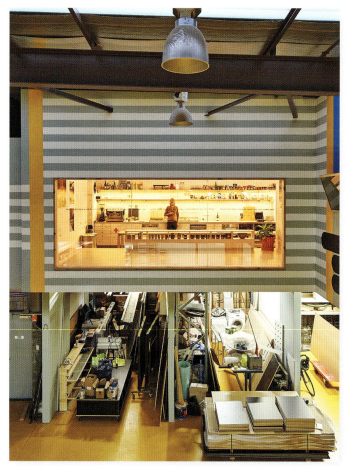

Just as in Garnier's Cité Industrielle, large-scale centres of production, logistics and distribution logically gravitate to their own peripheral zones, determined in part by connection to major infrastructure. Progressively fewer people need go there, and less often. With autonomous vehicles and autonomous factories, and AI's increased role in reading and learning from the gigabytes of data produced in the smart factory, an out-of-sight, out-of-mind, clearly zoned future awaits. Data power and AI optimise productivity and minimise resource use. Remote interfaces allow human design and development to take place in human-friendly environments, and production and distribution to take place in robot-friendly environments. The benefits of substantial computing capacity on the cloud mean that much of the workforce can, perhaps, spend more time at home.

Simultaneously, another scenario emerges in which the possibilities of Industry 4.0 for highly customised, just-in-time, small but high-value products facilitate fully distributed production. High-tech, small-volume, specialised high-value artisanal manufacturing thus returns in a new guise (a trend also observed in recent years). The factory in the garage quietly slips into the inner and outer suburbs and cohabits with the occupants of residential, now mixed-use areas, and into the back rooms of small-scale commercial shopping streets. Clean, quiet, sustainable, new digitalised production facilitates a fully integrated and distributed city of industry, local innovation, reduced transportation, proximity of production and consumption. Garnier's Cité Industrielle still serves well for the scale of metal refining, vehicle, aero, train, large battery manufacture and waste recycling, albeit with many of its worker inhabitants able to participate increasingly remotely, and prediction that even these activities may shrink and distribute. Conversely, the remixing of functions and zones through micro-manufacturing serves at a different scale of making to facilitate the much sought-after 20-minute walking neighbourhood.[5]

DYSTOPIC ALERT
Behold how Industry 4.0 and the exponential growth in internet traffic and cloud-based activity has spawned other large-scale, remote development sites with nothing urban about them. Consider the vast power-consumptive data warehouses in the Arizona desert, competing with local communities for precious water in a way reminiscent of the villain Dominic Greene in the James Bond film *Quantum of Solace* (2008).[4]

LLDS,
House 05,
Melbourne,
Australia,
2022

below: House 05 is a unique project for which LLDS utilised their Power to Make manufacturing arm to prototype and test their design from the mould insert for the in-situ concrete to the freeform laminated plywood roof beam. Advanced prototyping brings design closer to manufacturing and reduces the supply chain within an urban manufacturing context.

bottom: The design-to-manufacturing ethos of LLDS and Power to Make creates highly crafted and precise outcomes using advanced robotic fabrication techniques. Prefabricated architectural components such as the roof beams and brass roof lights are assembled on site using iterative point-cloud scanning to close the gap between the as-built structure and expected tolerance in design. Using augmented reality (AR) technology, LLDS checks the build quality against their digital model.

Leggett Loh Design Studio (LLDS)
and Power to Make,
Fink Street, Preston, Melbourne,
Australia,
2022

top: Combining design services, furniture making, fit-out fabrication, and product and production innovation, LLDS, Leggett and Loh's design consultancy, and Power to Make, their micro-manufacturing and digital fabrication facility, found a foothold in a small factory and residence in the middle suburb of Preston. Shown here are CNC-manufactured custom roof beams for an experimental house project. The location is critical to their creative production operation, allowing them to network not only with clients, but with other consultants, fabricators and suppliers.

bottom: LLDS's commissions have included bespoke furniture for Zaha Hadid Architects' Mayfair Residential Tower in Melbourne. They have seen other businesses squeezed out of the former industrial suburbs by rocketing land and rental values, some of whom have had to find ways to adapt to remote online working from the regions while they are committed to an urban model.

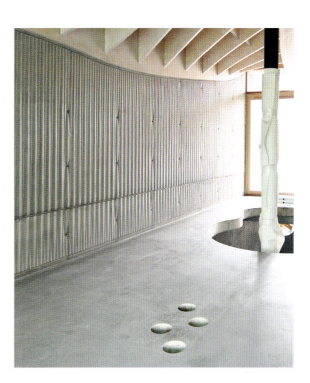

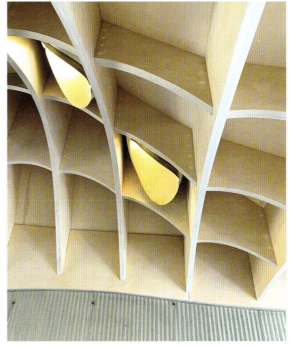

Connibere,
Grieve & Connibere hat factory,
Howard Street,
West Melbourne, Australia,
1906

While its Elizabethan-revival-style architecture is singular, this former factory is typical of the building type in the innermost suburbs of the city in its conversion to 'Howard West', an upmarket townhouse and apartment development. It is seen here with a large real-estate board promoting the sale of one of the units within. The rash of development of industrial land and buildings has increased residential density, week-round occupation and presence of cafes and restaurants, but at the cost of the small-scale manufacturing sector, which cannot compete with the gentrification.

At the same time, Industry 4.0 has sponsored the ubiquitous reintegration of productive activity into life at every scale, including the domestic, within cities that are otherwise growing and prospering. But what of the populations left behind? The decline of Detroit, Michigan, acts as an early harbinger of what the impact of the next wave of automation in the car industry, which has for generations supported whole cities in Germany, might be. In 2020, the German car industry employed 809,000 people,[6] a number that could easily be halved by 2030 with the shift to producing electric cars with six times fewer parts than their fossil-fuel counterparts, and much greater ease of full robotic automation of the manufacturing process.[7]

Car plants are major employers in more than 40 German cities and towns. But that is just one industry. The era of modernist zoning and agglomeration for all major industries carries not only a significant risk for local economies, but also the potential for commensurate damage to the social and urban fabric of towns and cities. Conversely, the invisible insidious nature of networked cyber-physical production, a world based on data, has already revealed its propensity for feeding greedily on the gig economy, enlisting online human workforces without the safeguards of formal employment. Even in developed countries, industrial relations and employment law is barely catching up, while the wealth and security divide grows and separates city populations.

But perhaps the greatest issue regarding industry in the post-Garnier city is the re-zoning, since 2000, of erstwhile inner-suburban industrial zones to mixed use. Understanding industrial space to be obsolete in a post-industrial economy driven by knowledge, finance and real estate, planning authorities opened these areas to mixed use with the laudable aim of housing people closer to work and services, and trying to arrest urban sprawl. But by the law of unintended consequences, by opening the door to property speculation and furious development and gentrification, this has driven out the new wave of specialist manufacturing, creative producers and small businesses underpinned by the Industry 4.0 revolution, and all the associated services. It has effectively reduced local employment.

Manufacturing in developed countries has changed. In Australia, for example, firms with fewer than 20 people represent more than 93 per cent of manufacturing employment, and three-quarters of firms have fewer than five employees. Variously facilitated by the nine cyber-physical pillars of

Industry 4.0, many of these are engaged in small-batch production of high-value-added and design-intensive products, often linked to cultural industries. They thrive in the dense human networks and consumer markets inside the city. Greater Melbourne alone has lost 2,423 hectares (the equivalent of 19 central business districts) of industrial zones since 2000, and this is a typical scenario.[8] So, while we witness new manifestations of exclusion and a crippling price paid for change by one of the most productive sectors of the population, the jury remains out on Garnier's zoning – time for a new zoning utopia for new industries, perhaps. ᴆ

Notes
1. Carl Benedikt Frey, *The Technology Trap: Capital Labor and Power in the Age of Automation*, Princeton University Press (Princeton, NJ), 2019.
2. William Blake, 'And did those feet in ancient time', poem in the preface to *Milton: A Poem in Two Books*, first published 1808: www.blakearchive.org/copy/milton.a?descId=milton.a.illbk.01.
3. Émile Zola, *Travail: les quatre évangiles*, Charpentier (Paris), 1901; translated into English as *Labour; a Novel*, Harper & Brothers (New York and London), 1901.
4. Marc Forster (director), *Quantum of Solace*, Eon Productions, 2008.
5. Lukar E Thornton *et al*, 'Operationalising the 20-Minute Neighbourhood', *International Journal of Behavioral Nutrition and Physical Activity*, 19 (1), 2022, pp 1–18: https://ijbnpa.biomedcentral.com/track/pdf/10.1186/s12966-021-01243-3.pdf.
6. Statista, 'Number of Employees in the Automobile Industry in Germany from 2010 to 2020', March 2021: www.statista.com/statistics/587576/number-employees-german-car-industry/.
7. 'How Car Manufacturing is Changing for EVs', *Automotive Daily*, 4 February 2022: www.autodaily.com.au/how-car-manufacturing-is-changing-for-evs/; Idaho National Laboratory, 'How Do Gasoline and Electric Vehicles Compare?': https://avt.inl.gov/sites/default/files/pdf/fsev/compare.pdf.
8. Carl Grodach, Chris Gibson and Justin O'Connor, 'Three Ways to Fix the Problems Caused by Rezoning Inner-city Industrial Land for Mixed-use Apartments', *The Conversation*, 26 August 2019: https://theconversation.com/three-ways-to-fix-the-problems-caused-by-rezoning-inner-city-industrial-land-for-mixed-use-apartments-121566.

THE GREATEST ISSUE REGARDING INDUSTRY IN THE POST-GARNIER CITY IS THE RE-ZONING, SINCE 2000, OF ERSTWHILE INNER-SUBURBAN INDUSTRIAL ZONES TO MIXED USE

Text © 2023 John Wiley & Sons Ltd. Images: © p 99(t) © Archives Charmet / Bridgeman Images; p 100(t) © March Studio; p 100(b) © March Studio, photo Peter Bennetts; p 101 © LLDS; pp 102–3 © Jane Burry

Kas Oosterhuis

Kas Oosterhuis with Ilona Lénárd, Yassmin Alkhasawneh, Hend Gamal and Yamamah Alsalloum,
Seven Daughters,
Qatar,
2020

The *Seven Daughters* is an event sculpture dedicated to the rise of feminine power in Qatar. The name is based on an old parable about the creation of the constellation Ursa Major. The sculpture has seven nodes, and the public navigates from node to node to experience today's version of the parable of the Seven Daughters.

ANOTHER NORMAL

A TECHNO-SOCIAL ALTERNATIVE TO TECHNO-FEUDAL CITIES

Innovator, writer, educator and practising designer **Kas Oosterhuis**, who leads the multidisciplinary innovation studio ONL [Oosterhuis_Lénárd], gives us a potted history of his urban inspirations – from architectural school with its preoccupation with linear urbanism and its speculative architecture precedents, to the great linear city being proposed in Saudi Arabia. The integration of computer technology has been crucial to ONL's substantial output and their quest for 'real-time' architecture and city planning that interacts with its inhabitants and adapts its fabric and form accordingly.

Kas Oosterhuis,
Strook door Nederland graduation project,
Delft University of Technology (TU Delft),
The Netherlands,
1979

Simple rules that create diversity and complexity are projected on the Strook door Nederland to create the specific character of the built environment inside the strip.

What is Utopia for one, is Dystopia for the other. The competition plan of Ivan Leonidov, a member of the Organisation of Contemporary Architects (OSA) group of Russian 'Disurbanists' and design leader of the linear city Magnitogorsk (1930),[1] stood diametrically opposed to that of the urbanists, led by the brothers Leonid, Viktor and Alexander Vesnin, who believed in planning new cities around industrial production centres. Leonidov opted for a superposition of settlements onto the landscape in a 25-kilometre (16-mile) long grid structure, featuring communal housing inside the strip and public buildings and leisure facilities loosely arranged in the surrounding landscape. This combination of abstraction and concreteness was a source of fascination to a Delft University of Technology (TU Delft) student of the 1970s. Leonodiv's Magnitogorsk did not at that time appear as a distant utopia, but as a practical solution to ease existing inequality issues. Yet, in the real world of the Soviet Stalinised revolution, as it was eventually built, the steel city Magnitogorsk was destined to become a workers' nightmare.

EXPLORING RULE-BASED LINEAR URBANISM

I was that student, and 'Strook door Nederland' (1979), the resulting graduation project, was a 200-kilometre (124-mile) long and 5-kilometre (3-mile) wide urban strip, part of a proposal for an urban scheme directly inspired by Magnitogorsk's original linear design. It was undertaken in ignorance of the fact that the Dutch architect Rem Koolhaas had also taken inspiration from the Russian Constructivists, although in a completely different manner. This is attested by his thesis project for the Architectural Association (AA) School of Architecture in 1972 – 'Exodus, or the voluntary Prisoners of Architecture', which depicts a walled linear city for voluntary prisoners imposed on the fabric of the City of London – and his 'Story of the Pool' project for the island of Manhattan (1978).[2] Koolhaas as an eloquent storyteller seemed more interested in the hedonism and heroism that formed part of the Russian constructivist thinking than in their social intentions and preference for new building technologies.

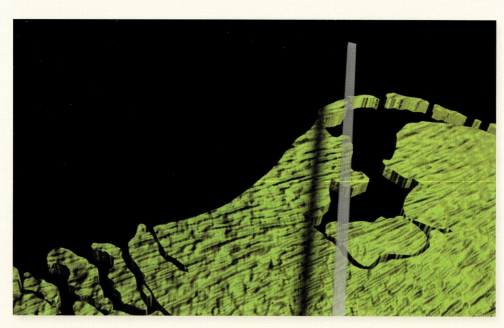

Ashok Bhalotra and Kas Oosterhuis,
City Fruitful,
Dordrecht,
the Netherlands,
1991

City Fruitful is a concrete experimental proposal for a city of 1,500 inhabitants consisting of about 1,700 homes and 30 hectares (74 acres) of greenhouses and outdoor cultivation, to create a symbiotic scheme of cultural, material and architectural hybridity. It produces its own food, recycles CO_2, and minimises the consumption of water and energy.

The Strook door Nederland is a form of rule-based urban design, exhibiting an interest in simple rules that generate complex outcomes, framed by the shape of the rule. The formal language of top-down rules and simple geometrical shapes is intended to create opportunities for bottom-up developments, wherein every inhabitant would have equal rights and opportunities. Usually, rules take the shape of a country; in the Strook, the rules of law govern within a given shape. The first rule is to allocate a generous piece of private land for the Dutch citizens inside the strip; which may sound radical, but land ownership has for decades been a birthright for their citizens in Middle Eastern countries. The second rule, in case the first rule would not pass the Dutch Parliament, is to abolish architectural guidelines – in the Netherlands called '*welstand*' – literally meaning 'in good standing' – both in terms of soundness and prosperity.

The Strook door Nederland is intentionally placed laterally to the main rivers and highways to establish many cross-connections. Crossing the Strook one would experience a temporary entry into another country with different rules, like crossing the border between Holland and Belgium. The basic idea is to democratise and thus normalise ubiquitous land ownership, demonstrating that other normal urban arrangements are as feasible as the current abnormal divide between social housing and luxurious villa parks.

CAR-FREE, FOOD-PRODUCING URBANISM

In 1991, a dozen years after the Strook, ONL [Oosterhuis_Lénárd] was formed to design the proposed masterplan for City Fruitful in Dordrecht, commissioned by the Dutch Spatial Planning Agency, an agro-metropolitan scheme for a car-free, food-producing, carbon-neutral city of 1,500 inhabitants.[3] The city's courtyard homes, pyramids, semi-detached and detached homes are all surmounted with custom-designed horticultural greenhouses that vary in size from small private ones to vast, collective robotised collective ones. Cars are parked in a multistorey car park, from where the CO_2 they produce is extracted and used by crops in the greenhouses. Water is conserved by modern drip-irrigation techniques; energy is saved by the use of thermal exchange between the greenhouses and dwellings below. City Fruitful was as concrete as it gets; no stories told, not a distant Utopia, but a precisely substantiated scheme based on the greenhouse experience of the Dutch farmer, on scientific facts and calculations by the energy consultant. It did not get enough political support back in 1991 for any level of realisation, however, let alone to become a beacon for a normality.

DIGITAL COMPONENTS FOR A GREEN CITY

In the late 1990s, ONL designed another city, also with 1,500 inhabitants: Reitdiep, north of Groningen. The parametric design instrument Attractor Game was developed to drag and drop the main constituent components into the digital working space. Attractor Game has water components, tree components, housing components and public components, and the masterplan is developed by carefully positioning the attractors and by setting the parameters. The purpose of Attractor Game is to make design decisions verifiable, quantifiable and qualifiable, based on simple rules that build optimal conditions for diversity. A series of sliders are used to vary the parameters for the attractors' strength and the area of influence. After placement of the attractors, a self-written routine scans the image, and translates the brightness of the coloured areas into quantified blocks proportional to the brightness. Thus, the total cubic metres of water, the total number of trees, the areas for housing and public facilities, and their coordinates, are known and form the basis for further design decisions. The housing domains form an archipelago of islands inside a smooth network of spacious green corridors. Stepping out of the backyard of the house means stepping directly into nature; the citizens can walk for kilometres without crossing a street. Bodies of water, trees, housing and public facilities are subsequently superimposed on top of each other and on top of the existing landscape, and overlap to form challenging new combinations. One particular home might be located on a water parcel and must take into account the trees that are planted before the house is built. Some simple design rules create the serendipitous diversity, as was intended in the Strook door Nederland, but taking a fluid, more complex shape.

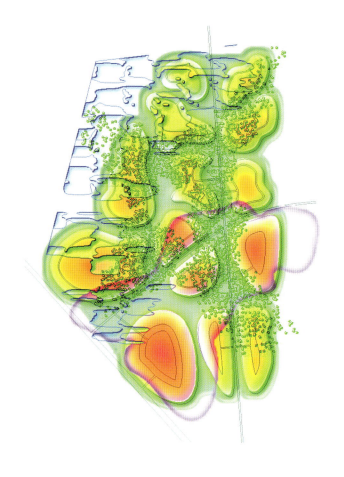

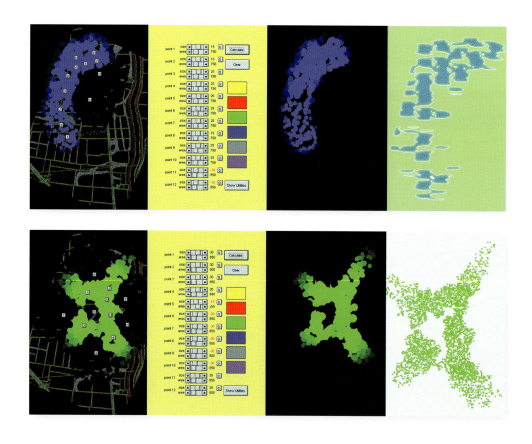

Kas Oosterhuis,
Attractor Game,
Reitdiep masterplan,
Groningen,
The Netherlands,
1998

top: The Attractor Game is played by a multidisciplinary team of stakeholders, setting the parameters for the area of influence and the strength of the attractors for surface water, trees, homes and public facilities.

middle: The masterplan is designed by dragging and dropping attractors into the working space, using sliders to set the parameters. Negative values turn attractors into repellers.

bottom: The housing attractors and repellers form an archipelago of neighbourhoods of various sizes. The continuous space in between the domains constitutes the city park.

Giò Forma studio,
Maraya concert hall,
Al-'Ula,
Saudi Arabia,
2019

Currently the world's largest mirrored building, in the heart of the town of Al-'Ula in the Saudi Arabian desert, the concert hall appears as a mesmerising fata morgana, a hardly tangible presence of an otherwise large structure. The cut-out entrance is clad in mirrored glass on all sides, giving the impression of stepping into another world.

NEOM CLAIMS TO BE ENVIRONMENTALLY FRIENDLY, APPLYING THE MOST MODERN TECHNOLOGIES TO CREATE AN ENVIRONMENT WITH ZERO CARS, ZERO STREETS AND ZERO CARBON EMISSIONS. TIME WILL TELL WHETHER IT CAN LIVE UP TO ITS AMBITIONS

A TECHNOLOGY-DRIVEN LINEAR CITY

In Saudi Arabia, a brand-new technology-driven city called NEOM[4] is under construction in Tabuk Province. The first phase is now scheduled to be completed in 2025, and it is projected to cover 26,500 square kilometres (10,232 square miles). The most challenging part of NEOM is The Line, a pedestrianised linear city serviced by underground infrastructure and a high-speed rail transport system that connects a series of neighbourhoods to create car-free, green urban environments reaching from the Gulf of Aqaba in the Red Sea to the Al Hejaz mountains and upper northwest valleys of the kingdom. The Line begins at the floating, octagonal industrial island Oxagon, in close proximity to Egypt and Israel to facilitate trade. At a location some 50 kilometres (31 miles) inland, in the mountains, NEOM is planning the luxury ski resort Trojena, featuring outdoor ski slopes and a canyon-shaped village.

The latest version of The Line compresses all buildings into one 170-kilometre (105-mile) long, 500-metre (1,640-foot) tall, 200-metre (656-foot) wide structure, both sides to be fully clad with mirrored glazing to reflect the surrounding desert and keep the interior science-fiction-style canyons cool. Seen in retrospect, the fully-mirrored building of the Maraya concert hall in Al-'Ula, in the same Tabuk region of Saudi Arabia, is a prototype for NEOM. NEOM claims to be environmentally friendly, applying the most modern technologies to create an environment with zero cars, zero streets and zero carbon emissions. Time will tell whether it can live up to its ambitions; as of now, the promotional videos and renderings show a libertarian alternative reality that is impossible to realise without a heavy environmental toll caused by the project's high levels of embodied carbon – in other words, business as usual, or as usual as it comes for the privileged.

The Line,
NEOM,
Saudi Arabia,
2022

right: In the apartment-lined canyon between the two 170-kilometre (105-mile) long mirror-clad, parallel, horizontal skyscrapers of NEOM is a diverse series of lushly planted science-fiction-style landscapes with overhanging balconies, waterfalls and trees.

below: The design plan for the 500-metre (1,640-foot) tall parallel structures, known collectively as The Line, forming the heart of the Red Sea megacity NEOM. The linear city will be clad entirely in mirrored glass, as was trialled recently in the Maraya concert hall in Al-'Ula, Saudi Arabia, which reflects the surrounding expanse of unspoilt desert while helping maintain cool temperatures within.

THE PROPOSED ANOTHER NORMAL IS NOT A SPECULATIVE UTOPIA, BUT AN UNCOMPROMISING IMPLEMENTATION OF AVAILABLE TECHNOLOGY IN SYNC WITH CURRENT TRENDS AND DEVELOPMENTS

A WORKING HYPOTHESIS FOR A FEASIBLE TECHNO-SOCIAL UTOPIA

The concept espoused for Another Normal,[5] loosely based on the brilliant techno-social fiction novel *Another Now* by Yannis Varoufakis (2021),[6] would entail several simple rules, rolled out to form the basis for a substantiated new approach for urban planning, and applying the most effective digital technologies for efficient, zero-carbon emissive worldmaking. Based on the design strategy of 'simplexity', meaning simple rules that create diversity and complexity, a limited number of socio-technical rules for a more fair and just society are proposed: 1) introduce universal basic income for all inhabitants within the planned city, to guarantee they have the means to develop themselves; 2) grant the inhabitants the unalienable right to own and use a plot of land of generous size; 3) produce at least one-third of the inhabitants' needs for food, water and energy in their own houses and on their own land, whereas the other two-thirds are delivered by the neighbourhood, city or country; 4) request parametric design for robotic production for all the inhabitants' consumer goods, including their homes, while the production facilities must be as close as possible to their homesteads; 5) complete reliance on automated electric vehicles for transport within the city; and 6) all consumer products purchased from outside the city to be delivered by robotic delivery services.

These six simple, strong conceptual rules will create an unheard-of diversity and complexity, while securing a fair and just society, and are feasible using existing technologies. The fourth rule has been extensively elaborated in several built projects. For the Saltwater Pavilion (1997), at Burgh-Haamstede, a radical file-to-factory process was developed, whereby the output data of the design are used as input data for computer-numerically-controlled (CNC) machines. The iWEB protoSPACE, originally designed as a pavilion for the province of Noord Holland at the 2002 horticultural exposition Floriade, was the first building to be built in its totality according to the principles of applying parametric design to robotic production. The A2 Cockpit and the Acoustic Barrier (2005) along the A2 highway from Amsterdam to Maastricht, meant the definitive breakthrough of CNC-driven design-to-production methods on a larger scale. The recent *Seven Daughters* sculpture (2022) in Qatar, and the Netherlands pavilion at Dubai Expo (2018) are based in their entirety on one single, all-inclusive parametric detail, with structure and skin synchronised into one coherent system referred to as the 'One Building, One Detail' strategy. They represent the ultimate aesthetic of the Another Normal, where all building components are unique in shape and performance, the designs are parametric and the production robotic.

The proposed Another Normal is not a speculative Utopia, but an uncompromising implementation of available technology in sync with current trends and developments. The rules of law are bound to the shape of the target area only, leaving the rest of the country unaffected. Naturally, the appeal of another real, existing normal will eventually affect the whole country. The six rules, combined, aim to form a concrete counterbalance to supposedly libertarian, 'techno-feudal' alternative realities such as NEOM or Liberland. A micronation on disputed land between Croatia and Serbia, the Free Republic of Liberland was proclaimed in 2015 by the right-libertarian politician Vit Jedlička. The futuristic urban planning and design of Zaha Hadid Architects' Liberland Metaverse virtual city (2022) replicates the physical landmass of this disputed location while functioning as a free-standing virtual realm in its own right.[7] In the 'techno-social' Another Normal, the connections between people and things will be verifiably quantified and qualified to reduce the carbon footprint of the city while ruling out the pernicious division between haves and have-nots. △

NOTES
1. Andrei Gozak and Andrei Leonidov, *Ivan Leonidov: The Complete Works*, Academy Editions (London), 1988, pp 87–93.
2) Rem Koolhaas and Madelon Vriesendorp, 'Story of the Pool', appendix to *Delirious New York: A Retroactive Manifesto for Manhattan*, Oxford University Press (Oxford), 1978, pp 307–11.
3. Gijs Wallis de Vries (ed), *City Fruitful*, Uitgeveri 010 Publishers (Rotterdam), 1991.
4. NEOM, Tabuk province, Saudi Arabia: www.neom.com.
5. Kas Oosterhuis, *The Component: A Personal Odyssey Towards Another Normal*, work in progress.
6. Yannis Varoufakis, *Another Now*, The Bodley Head / Penguin Random House (London), 2020.
7. Zaha Hadid Architects, Masterplan for Liberland Metaverse, 2022: www.archdaily.com/978522/zaha-hadid-architects-designs-cyber-urban-metaverse-city.

Kas Oosterhuis, Netherlands Pavilion, Expo 2020 Dubai, 2020

The design is an example of the 'One Building, One Detail' strategy, in which the structure and skin form a system based on one parametric detail that is directly linked to the robotic production of its constituent components.

Text © 2023 John Wiley & Sons Ltd. Images: pp 104, 106, 108–9, 111 © Kas Oosterhuis; p 107 © Kuiper Compagnons; p 110 © NEOM

THE FLOATING

NLÉ Architects,
Makoko water community of tomorrow,
Lagos, Nigeria,
2014

A proposal for Makoko with a new, expanded linear system of waterways for transport and floating mobile markets, allowing for transient programmes such as food production and community workshops. The new urban block typology is organised around a hybrid infrastructure, prioritising circulation and adaptation and defence against rising sea levels.

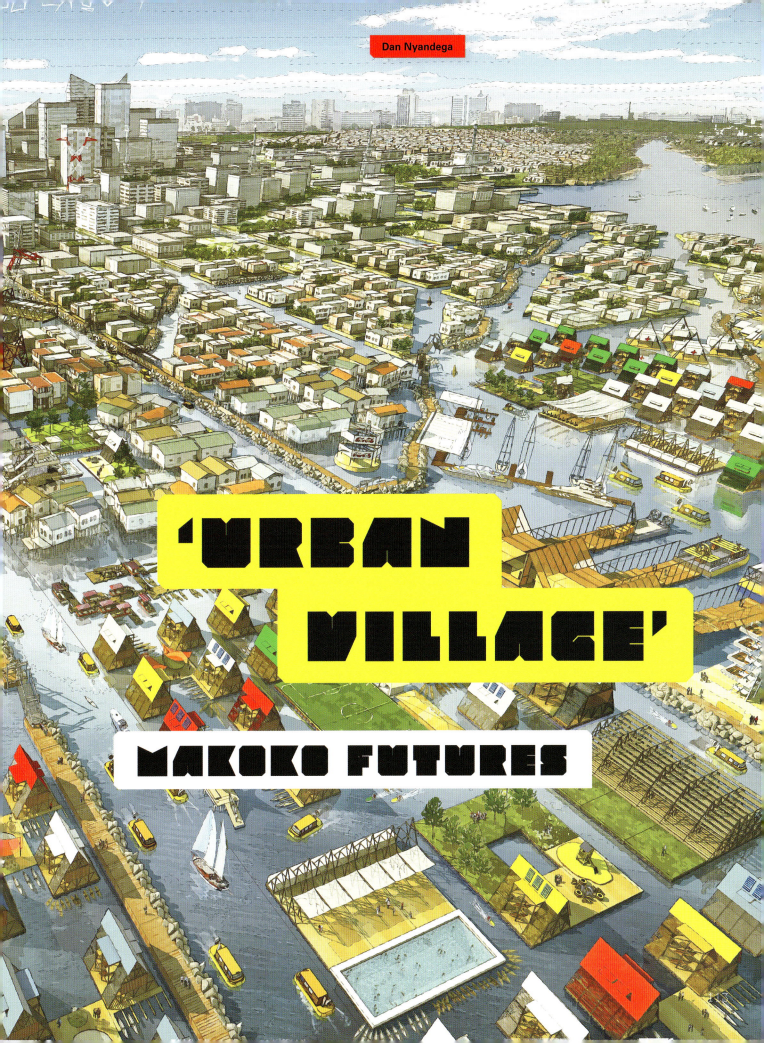

Our current climate condition means that we need to start developing better tactics, protocols and new building typologies that mitigate water shortages or are resilient to flood situations. **Dan Nyandega** is a lecturer in Landscape Architecture and Urbanism at Queensland University of Technology (QUT) in Brisbane, Australia. He has a PhD in architecture (water-sensitive design) from Monash University, Melbourne, and his design-led research explores the intersection of coastal cities' infrastructures, landscapes, architecture and rising water levels. He takes as small case studies Makoko on the Lagos Lagoon and Kenzō Tange's Tokyo Bay Project of 1960, but also warns of the potential loss of authenticity and genius loci with such interventions.

Coastal cities face threats from rising sea levels, floods, lack of room for expansion, housing shortages and high land costs. In the past, the responses to these challenges have been lofty and, in some cases, utopian. In an era of rapidly increasing urban populations and accelerated climate change, some of the more utopian proposals from the past century such as Kenzō Tange's 1960 Plan for Tokyo, and French architect and urban planner Paul Maymont's Thalassa and the Utopia of the Floating City project for the extension of Monaco (1963) have renewed relevance. Several more recent responses, such as the Makoko Floating System (MFS™, 2011) scheme for the water community of Makoko, in Lagos, Nigeria, by Kunlé Adeyemi of NLÉ Architects, have also sketched out utopian design proposals. However, while these optimistic schemes have the potential to translate into reality, they could also go wrong.

Contemporary Urban Challenges: Makoko
Makoko is an informal floating 'urban village' on the waterfront of the Lagos Lagoon. It began as six distinct fishing villages approximately 200 years ago and is now home to a population of up to 300,000. Over the last 100 years the settlement has sprawled out about half a mile into the marshy, shallow lagoon[1] but is still not legally recognised by the government. Even as it simultaneously battles for legitimacy and against rising water levels and more frequent storms,[2] Makoko is under constant threat of demolition for redevelopment by the Lagos State Government.

Problems related to Makoko's unplanned growth have been exacerbated by small-scale land reclamation and the rampant and spontaneous construction of individual dwellings made out of timber, reused waste materials and assembled by locals with skills developed over decades. Because this expansion is carried out in the absence of a government-sanctioned support system, the quality of the land reclamation is uneven and the houses stand precariously on wooden stilts sunk into the saline tidal mudflats at an average depth of half a metre. The structures are always at risk of sinking as they are susceptible to rising water levels and storm surges. Makoko's residents act out of necessity, as they lack any alternative but to attempt to grow out of their extreme situation collectively, creatively and incrementally.

Makoko water community, Lagos, Nigeria, 2019

What appear to be clusters of individual buildings emerge as a collective project of houses on stilts. The settlement's expansion into a territory not explored by the formal city forms a collective territorial and micro-scale logic and urban structure informed by a labyrinth of waterways for canoe transport and mobile markets, defying that of the larger city while offering clues to the future of cities in low-lying areas.

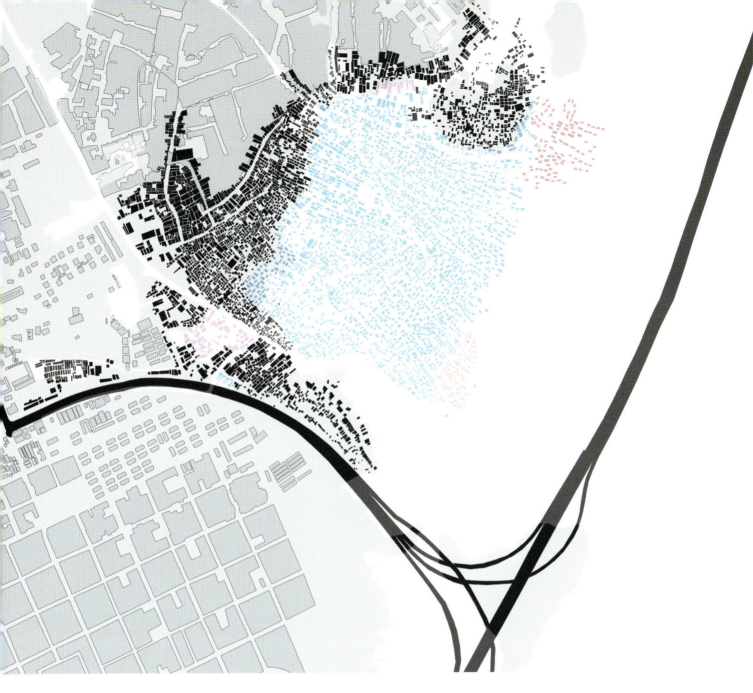

Dan Nyandega,
Mapping Makoko,
Lagos, Nigeria,
2020

above: Makoko informal floating city (in blue) sprawls into the muddy shallows of Lagos Lagoon within a few hundred yards of modern buildings. The building footprints in red are areas which underwent episodes of demolition by the Lagos State Government in 2019. The government considers the settlement an impediment to the development of the waterfront, and has repeatedly attempted to raze it.

Makoko,
Remnants of demolition,
Lagos, Nigeria,
2019

left: Makoko residents salvaging wooden remnants of their stilt houses demolished by the Lagos State Government in 2019. The wooden remnants were reused for reconstruction within the settlement.

A Utopian Scheme

NLÉ Architects' scheme for the Makoko water community began in 2012 as an A-framed building for a floating school, which later collapsed due to extreme storms.[3] As a response to exponential urbanisation, housing shortages and the effects of climate change in coastal cities, the A-framed building nevertheless became a prototype that would inform utopic speculation for architecture and urbanism of the settlement. NLÉ's scheme became part of their wider 'African Water Cities' project that has now been extended and tested in other cities, including Venice (2016), Bruges (2018), Chengdu (2018) and Mindelo, Cape Verde in 2021.[4] Recognising the way its inhabitants have responded to the challenges they face, the scheme draws inspiration from Makoko as an innovative, economical and contemporary model for African coastal cities. It explores the urban village as a repository of clues for developing future solutions while attempting to strengthen its identity as a place where water remains an asset for the local fishing community rather than being exploited by real-estate developers as a feature in luxury developments for the wealthy.

The Makoko Floating System building prototype creates a replicable system of floating housing that is adaptable, moveable and economically self-sufficient, suitable in Makoko and many other expanding communities and new cities on water.[5] The units are modular, scalable, and designed in three sizes: small, medium and large, with one, two and three floors respectively, with different internal configurations to create adaptable spaces that can be used as floating homes or large cultural halls.

NLÉ's scheme offers flexibility for residents to construct their own houses using local and reused or repurposed materials, community skills and labour to reduce costs. The overall plan designates the ground level of individual houses as public space to facilitate commercial activity, recreation, workshops and social activities. The houses are arranged in groups of four units with a central communal space linked to the public areas on the ground floor of each house to catalyse social interaction with neighbours. The shared ground levels create a continuum with the shared water territory. On an urban scale, the settlement is structured along widened linear waterways for water transport and mobile markets, adapted from the existing labyrinth of waterways and continuing its distinct legacy from the larger city. Building on the existing idiom of small-scale land reclamation in the settlement, it proposes strategic micro-islands for urban activities that require dry land, such as parks and sports fields. The project's structure will facilitate continuous expansion and dynamic public programming along the linear corridors, effectively creating diverse social and commercial activities as required by the community. Such programmes include workshops, markets, playgrounds, and floating vegetable- and fish farms to bolster the fishing community.

Relevant Again

While climate change was not a major discourse at the time of Tange's and Maymont's plans, some of the challenges witnessed in contemporary coastal cities resemble those addressed in Tange's 1960 Tokyo Bay project, evoking a renewed interest in such 20th-century proposals. Tange's plan came at a time when many cities in the industrial world were experiencing

NLÉ Architects,
Makoko Floating System (MFS),
Mindelo, Cape Verde,
2021

opposite: An example of the MFS building prototype, adapted as a floating music hub. The prefabricated self-build system comes in several sizes, with configurable inner spaces, and offers a way of addressing housing issues and climate-change challenges experienced by waterfront communities.

Marcus White and Tashleigh van Graan,
Adaptation of Kenzō Tange's 1960 Plan for Tokyo,
2022

below: The New Urban Structure Order is a megastructure made up of interlocking linear structures, expanding the city across Tokyo Bay, an area not previously considered for development, effectively offering access to new districts.

unrestricted urban sprawl. As a response, he proposed imposing a new physical order on Tokyo which would accommodate the city's continued expansion and internal regeneration. Unlike Maymont's scheme of an imposing circular shell for the Thalassa Monaco extension, Tange proposed a shift away from the existent radial zoning status towards a linear development in the form of a megastructure, and a spatial order with greater relevance to Makoko. The plan offered a 'fixed' transport infrastructure composed of highways and subways that allowed for transient urban programming dictated by the population's individual needs. The megastructure would begin as a series of columns to support the buildings, freeing the ground space to become shared spatial territory. The columns would serve as service cores, access points and urban structural elements, allowing the rest of the above-ground spaces to continually evolve and decentralise as required.

At the time, the scheme was a new approach to urban sprawl and still remains relevant for its goal of providing individual experiences, flexibility, access and expediency to major parts of the city. In addition to exploring the city as an ongoing process with continuous relationships between permanence and ephemerality, it also emphasised some major urban concepts including urban structure, mobility and the civic axis.[6] While Tange's approach to these concepts was utopian and symbolic rather than pragmatic, their potential translation into reality remains germane in discussions about urban development in current and near-future cities. Similarly, although conceived for a vastly different geographical, economic and cultural context and time, the challenges faced and the solutions he proposed are especially relevant to Makoko.

From Ideal to Reality

When moving from the grand display of utopian visions to the reality of creating a viable urban proposal for a settlement such as Makoko, it is necessary to be cognisant of the low-income community's context, ethos and governance system. In Makoko, a new physical order might be a well-defined water transport corridor. This fixed infrastructure would require only minimal and incremental intervention. It would allow for continuous expansion and flexibility to strengthen the existing community and individual agency manifested in the settlement's construction of stilt houses. Transient urban programming would then thrive, dictated by the community, housing clusters and individual interventions. Makoko's existential situation would transition from one of impermanence driven by fear and the threat of eviction, characterised by precariously built stilt houses, to a positive kind of impermanence dictated by the community's needs and characterised by regeneration and resilient houses.

Freeing the ground level as a shared spatial territory, as was done by Tange, has been reinterpreted as a response to rising water levels in Makoko in Adeyemi's scheme. Makoko's existing, unique, community-driven expansion has thrived on what can be interpreted as assumed collective ownership of the shallow water by the community, albeit illegally. Shallow water in Makoko is deemed a 'fluid' ground on which to live, build on and carry out socioeconomic activities, and also as a source of raw materials. Out of necessity, the ubiquitous presence of water is accepted as merely a different surface material on which to dwell. Their 'ground' is fluid, wet and collectively owned. This collective approach deemed the available shallow water as an alternative to the city's expensive and overly privatised dry land, with its restrictive and ubiquitous property boundaries and unattainable to the community. The shallow waters of the lagoon became a public space and a community asset, challenging the now-perversive exploitation of water as a real-estate asset at the expense of the local waterfront communities.

While Adeyemi's scheme also alludes to this collective ownership, its long-term practicality involves complex challenges for the community's system of governance. It suggests a break from restrictive and ubiquitous private property boundaries to strengthen the existing collective ownership. This aligns with the understanding that water problems are community problems, because water knows no property boundaries, ownership or jurisdictions. By the same token, shared water can be an effective tool with which to rally the community around the challenges posed by rising water levels and pollution. The scheme's success would require a radical shift in governance that would depend on the willingness of local government to put in place administrative systems to support legalised but controlled collective ownership of the lagoon territory by the community. However, this would have to be done in such a way as to protect the local residents, the fishing community, and enhance the productivity of the territory while repairing the fragile lagoon ecosystem.

Amidst what appears to an outsider's eye to be a dystopic environment – messy and chaotic, with polluted water and human health and welfare problems – over the decades Makoko has developed its own uniquely complex rationales and forms of collective intelligence. Some of these resemble elements of the idealistic schemes created by visionaries of the past, and would only need to be revealed, emboldened and made more deliberate. Some examples of such elements are: the local community-driven urban expansion outside restrictive government systems; housing typologies that coexist with water; small-scale, incremental interventions such as land reclamation using waste materials; and expansion into territories not explored by the formal city. Collectively, they have a cumulative effect and are dictated by the community's needs. In other words, some of the concepts that may seem ideal in other contexts already exist in Makoko.

While the ideal is often associated with grand and lofty propositions, Makoko shows us that aspects of it already exist in some of the most unlikely places, waiting to be revealed. In addition to formalising existing positive aspects by learning from past utopic schemes, Makoko's future can also be reimagined by looking inwards, tactfully revealing, strengthening and building on the existing logic of its collective response to external threats, urban expansion, land and housing shortages, issues of mobility, rising water levels and water pollution. Makoko, in many respects, is an analogue to utopic future scenarios. It offers alternative clues for how to adjust to seemingly dystopic future land- and housing-shortage scenarios and the ubiquitous presence of water due to rising sea levels. However, these utopic ideas could potentially result in disbenefits once translated into reality.

> For cities to avoid the potential disbenefit of any improvement schemes, the translation of ideals into reality must be highly contextualised, community-driven, and built on the existing logic of settlement, processes and systems of governance

Dystopic Disbenefits

Translating ideal propositions into reality comes with risks if not contextualised. The urban village could become appealing, expensive and a romanticised tourist trap, effectively displacing the local communities that would no longer be able to afford to live in Makoko and similar waterfront settlements. Such gentrification would also result in further marginalisation and the mushrooming of similar waterfront settlements in other locations to accommodate the displaced people. A settlement's desirability also has the potential to shift its economy from community-driven fishing and small-scale timber-cutting to an economy dependent on tourism. This might result in community members renting out their floating houses or sharing them with outsiders (Airbnb), injection of tourist-focused restaurants, recreational fishing and theme-park-type water recreation. Such increased activities and population would also increase pressure on the fragile ecosystem. Collectively, they would rid the settlement of its authenticity, making it generic and undermining its centuries-long social structure and cultural ties to a water-based economy and governance system. The community would lose control of the settlement with potential privatisation pressure from the wealthy outsiders. Makoko as we know it would incrementally lose its authenticity and ties to the place.

For cities to avoid the potential disbenefit of any improvement schemes, the translation of ideals into reality must be highly contextualised, community-driven, and built on the existing logic of settlement, processes and systems of governance. Any new proposal must show local leaders the untapped possibilities that are currently considered urban challenges. Rather than focusing on the unattainability of utopian ideas or our failure to construct them, understanding such visions from the position of their timely relevance while keeping in mind the potential disbenefits of their translation into reality would make them realisable. ᗞ

Notes
1. Jonathan Glancey, 'Learning from Lagos', *Architectural Review*, 234 (1399), 2013, pp 64–71.
2. Sharon Ogunleye, 'Floating School in Lagos Lagoon Collapses Under Heavy Rains', Reuters, 8 June 2016: www.reuters.com/article/us-nigeria-school-idUSKCN0YU26W.
3. Cynthia Okoroafor, 'Does Makoko Floating School's Collapse Threaten the Whole Slum's Future?', *The Guardian*, 10 June 2016: www.theguardian.com/cities/2016/jun/10/makoko-floating-school-collapse-lagos-nigeria-slum-water.
4. NLÉ Architects, African Water Cities Project, 2011–: www.nleworks.com/case/african-water-cities-project/.
5. NLÉ Architects and Heinrich Böll Stiftung, 'Makoko Floating School', Research Report, April 2012: http://www.nleworks.com/publication/makoko-research-heinrich-boll-stiftung/.
6. ArchEyes, 'A Plan for Tokyo 1960/Kenzō Tange', 26 January 2016: https://archeyes.com/plan-tokyo-1960-kenzo-tange/.

NLÉ Architects,
Makoko Floating System (MFS),
Minjiang Water City,
China,
2018

Three modular prototypes are scaled and adapted as an open-air concert hall, an indoor exhibition space and a small information centre clustered around a communal plaza.

Text © 2023 John Wiley & Sons Ltd. Images: pp 112–13, 116–17(t), 118–19 © NLÉ Architects; pp 114, 115(b) © Iwan Baan; p 115(t) © Dan Nyandega; pp 116–17(b) © Marcus White and Tashleigh van Graan

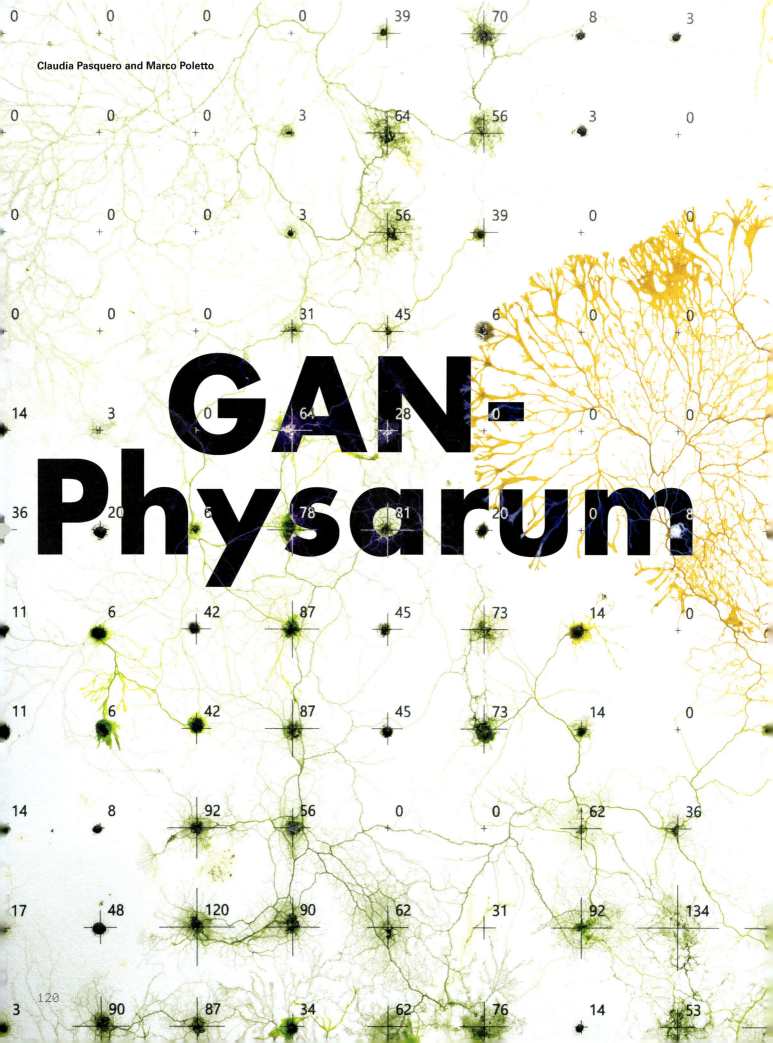

Claudia Pasquero and Marco Poletto

GAN-Physarum

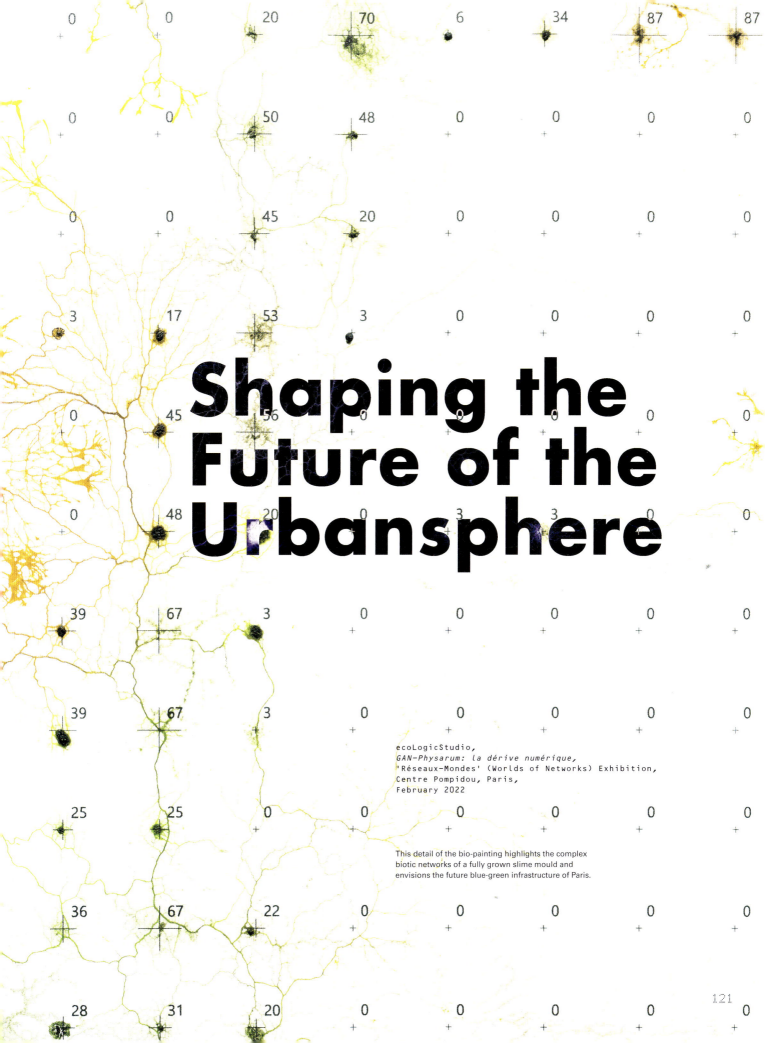

Shaping the Future of the Urbansphere

ecoLogicStudio,
GAN-Physarum: la dérive numérique,
'Réseaux-Mondes' (Worlds of Networks) Exhibition,
Centre Pompidou, Paris,
February 2022

This detail of the bio-painting highlights the complex biotic networks of a fully grown slime mould and envisions the future blue-green infrastructure of Paris.

Co-founders of the London architectural practice ecoLogicStudio, **Claudia Pasquero and Marco Poletto** have long been interested in the bio-digital, the synthesis between biology, computer algorithms and machine learning. In this article they describe and discuss their recent project GAN-Physarum, in effect a virtual slime mould creating a modern take on Constant Nieuwenhuys's visionary New Babylon project (1956–74) and its dérives, and unleashed on a virtual Paris.

The GAN-Physarum is a man-made bio-digital algorithm and a generative bio-computational network based on training a machine-learning algorithm to behave like a living slime mould, and subsequently deployed to depict the future of a bio-digital, autonomous Paris. This vision was developed in conversation with Centre Pompidou curators Marie-Ange Brayer and Olivier Zeitoun for their series of annual cross-disciplinary events entitled 'Mutations / Créations' (2017–) that focus on the interaction of digital technology and creation. GAN-Physarum questions the place of the network in our societies, its pervasiveness as well as its dematerialisation, and was part of the exhibition 'Réseaux-mondes', the fifth edition of 'Mutations / Créations', which took place in 2022.

The network is at the heart of technological change and several societal issues: surveillance, atomisation of the individual, actor-network relationships, AI and the emergence of the global urbansphere: 'Against this backdrop, we are witnessing the unfolding of a post-natural history, a time when the impact of artificial systems on the natural biosphere is indeed global, but their agency is no longer entirely human. Cities like Paris have become co-evolving networks of biological and digital intelligence, semi-autonomous synthetic organisms.'[1]

Bio-digital Networks

Technically, a GAN (generative adversarial network) is an algorithmic architecture that creates new generative models using deep-learning methods. ecoLogicStudio trained this powerful form of artificial intelligence to 'behave' like a *Physarum polycephalum*, a single-celled slime mould. When the trained GAN-Physarum is sent on a computational dérive, or 'drift', through the streets of Paris, it reveals how to decode and reinterpret the gridded patterns of the contemporary city into a smooth urban landscape. A transition from the original morphological order to an emergent distributed network of evolving path systems is witnessed.

The sequence, captured and brought to life in a computational time-lapse video, is accompanied by a corresponding bio-painting, approximately one square metre in size, where the living *Physarum polycephalum* stretches its networked body to feed on a grid of nutrients, distributed on the canvas to accurately map the current Parisian biotic resources. The traces of its path at such high resolution on the canvas are the embodiment of the slime mould's cognitive system, and create a non-human narrative of a completely different urban structure – Paris's very own evolving biotechnological brain. It is perhaps impossible to capture this vision with words or a single image, therefore the value of GAN-Physarum is to provide an instrument with which to model it.

The Utopia of New Babylon

In the visual artist Constant Nieuwenhuys' words: 'Thinking about a social structure that is so different from the existing one that it can safely be called its antithesis, words and terms are inadequate tools. Since what we are considering here is no abstraction but the material world, as in physics, it seems most logical to resort to visual tools, in other words a model.'[2]

In Constant's case this model was called New Babylon, the extraordinary tale of a global city devoted to playfulness and creativity. Conceived in the 1960s as an original view of a new way of life, the fictitious city was the product of a hyper-connected society that has reached freedom from responsibility thanks to its extraordinary apparatus of mechanical urban devices. While the machines handled all hard labour and productive work, New Babylon's population could indulge in an entirely ludic lifestyle.

The *homo ludens* of this society was a creative, nomadic and free person. In New Babylon, this freedom allows for continuous movement and the possibility of living in a season-less, timeless, boundless, limitless environment. This aspect of nomadic life, according to French authors Gilles Deleuze and Félix Guattari, allows the inhabitation of a homogeneous smooth space as opposed to the organised striated space of the gridded city.[3] Moreover, nomadic space is haptic, associative, interconnected – just like the world the slime mould navigates.

ecoLogicStudio,
GAN-Physarum: la dérive numérique,
'Réseaux-Mondes' (Worlds of Networks) Exhibition,
Centre Pompidou, Paris,
February 2022

top left: Overview of the *GAN-Physarum: la dérive numerique* exhibition. A machine-learning algorithm was trained to exhibit the behaviour of a living slime mould in re-imagining the future of an autonomous bio-digital Paris.

above: In this bio-painting for the exhibition, the slime mould was grown on canvas onto which nutrients were distributed according to a protocol derived from a satellite analysis of the current biotic structure of Paris.

left: Video projection for the 'Réseaux-Mondes' exhibition. The animated sequence was produced entirely with an AI algorithm. It depicts the evolving urban fabric of Paris in 100 years as envisioned by the biological intelligence of a living slime mould.

Physarum Polycephalum

Slime moulds – formerly classified as fungi but now grouped within the kingdom Protista – are monocellular organisms with a peculiar body composed of thousands of nuclei, afloat in a sea of globular, multifunctional proteins called actin, enclosed by a single stretchy membrane. From this, they derive their unique morphing properties. The *Physarum polycephalum*'s first dérive took place in the air-conditioned laboratories of the Synthetic Landscape Lab at the University of Innsbruck. Here, at a constant room temperature of 20°C (68°F), a living *Physarum polycephalum* in its active plasmodium phase hunted for nutrients within the sterile environment of a borosilicate glass Petri dish.

The process starts with a searching phase during which the pulsating body branches out in all directions to seek out food sources and their relative distribution and size. What follows is a phase of optimisation. Finely detailed branches emerge in the relevant areas of the Petri dish while areas without food sources are abandoned. Eventually, some of the branches grow in size and become thickening, convoluted transportation arteries. The optimised configuration never settles, however. As resources diminish and their overall distribution changes, the *Physarum polycephalum*'s morphology adjusts in real time.

The scarcer the resources become, the more change and adaptation accelerate. At the tipping point, the *Physarum polycephalum* is seen racing around the Petri dish in an attempt to find new food sources that will provide it with sufficient energy to sustain its searching efforts. Once nothing is left it retreats, devoting all remaining energy to creating new fruiting bodies, thus commencing the next phase in its uniquely elaborate life cycle.

On a philosophical level, through the reinterpretation of Constant's concept of New Babylon, GAN-Physarum is an investigation into Guy Debord's theory of 'la dérive'[4] and the effects of non-human psycho-geography on the perception of the city. Then, as now, performing dérive experiments and documenting the trajectories of the routes allows for a new interpretation of zones as vortices, areas of differential tension present in the liquefied space of the city. In the slime mould, the spatial vortices have the ability to contract and expand, which is a result of the peristaltic flow within the liquid space of its body. The shifting of the floating nuclei in the slime mould's body can be related back to the behaviour of *homo ludens*, the inhabitant of Constant's New Babylon. Both are encouraged to create their own environments and situations.

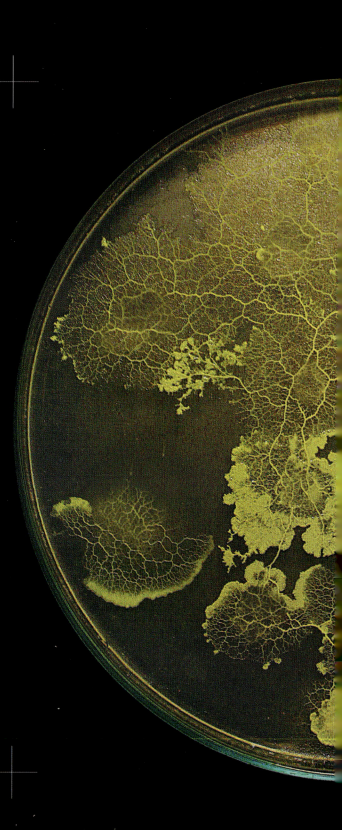

ecoLogicStudio,
slime mould used in GAN-Physarum: la dérive numérique,
Bc16 Urban Morphogenesis Lab, Bartlett School of Architecture, University College London (UCL),
2022

Macro-detail of a living *Physarum polycephalum* slime mould grown in a Petri dish on nutritious agar – a form of gelatine derived from seaweed that can be infused with various nutrients. The set-up allows deployment of slime mould as a biological computer to train AI algorithms.

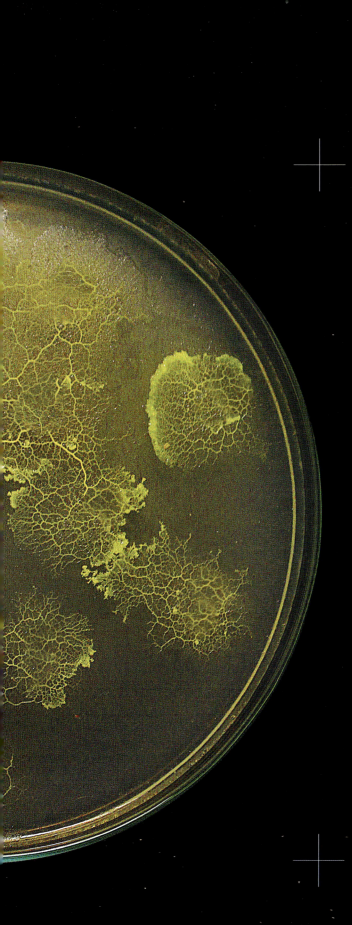

La Dérive Numérique

In GAN-Physarum's experiment, the main Parisian dérive began with a satellite image of Paris, duly processed to extract information about its biotic layer (plants, grasses, rivers and other 'wet' surfaces), and remapped onto a physical grid to provide an exact distribution of nutrient density. The points on the grid transfer the corresponding latitudinal and longitudinal geo-data of the map of Paris onto a canvas. A 3D data matrix is compiled, storing the density of biomass as a percentage value of a fully vegetated pixel. These density percentages are translated proportionally into quantities of nutrients on the *Physarum polycephalum* growth canvas, with a cell size of 3 cm (1.20 inches). *Physarum polycephalum* was then introduced, to begin its long bio-computational process.

Similarly, in New Babylon, the nomad moves in an artificial, wholly constructed environment, where social mobility builds a kaleidoscope of events that are divided between the city's sectors. Elaborate systems of transportation are important to facilitate freedom of movement between the sectors. However, instead of tools for work they become tools for play. One navigates the boundless city of New Babylon using psycho-geography, the practice of a subjective apprehension of space. Environmental and social comfort and even happiness come into play. Whether consciously or not, the environment is registered and reorganised from a series of geographical and physical fragments, individual emotions and affects.

In the original New Babylon, comfort was a result of detachment from natural climate and independence from diurnal rhythms and seasons. It was life envisioned in artificially lit spaces and stable ambient temperature. In reality, even small changes in environmental conditions are registered and perceived as subjective phenomena resulting, by default, in altered space. Thus, air conditioning not only serves to re-create an ideal climate, as it does in an utilitarian society, but to provide the greatest possible variation of ambiance.

New Babylon was Constant's proposal for the Situationists' response to the city. Traditional architecture, as a result, has disintegrated in Constant's vision and has been replaced with a vast network of multilayered spaces and sectors which would eventually cover the whole planet in an endless urbansphere.[5] In GAN-Physarum, AI was deployed to model a vision for an autonomous bio-digital city, made for both human and non-human citizens and planned by a new form of non-human intelligence.

GAN-Physarum deploys a machine-learning technique that uses the training of image-to-image translation models without paired examples. A GAN has two parts, the generator and the discriminator, engaged in an internal competition. The generator learns to generate plausible data. The generated instances become negative training examples for the discriminator. The discriminator learns to distinguish the generator's fake data from real data. The discriminator penalises the generator for producing implausible results.[6]

GAN Physarium Paris
Growth: 20
Scale: 10 Km
Building transformation: 15118

GAN Physarium Paris
Growth: 70
Scale: 1 Km
Building transformation: 55256

GAN Physarium Paris
Growth: 86
Scale: 200 m
Building transformation: 67833

ecoLogicStudio,
GAN-Physarum: la dérive numérique,
'Réseaux-Mondes' (Worlds of
Networks) exhibition,
Centre Pompidou, Paris,
February 2022

top left: Video still from the AI simulation of *Physarum polycephalum's* exploratory activity. The 10-kilometre (6-mile) frame of the urban fabric of Paris envisions the rearranged blue-green infrastructures of the entire city centre, as derived from the slime mould's intelligent search for nourishment.

top right: This 1-kilometre (0.62-mile) frame of Paris's urban fabric as explored by the AI algorithm modelled on the behaviour of *Physarum polycephalum* proposes a new urban massing for the Beaubourg neighbourhood.

bottom: The 100-metre (32-foot) frame showing the *Physarum polycephalum's* simulated activity depicts a new bio-digital Centre Pompidou, its architectural apparatus now re-engineered into a soft and wet living network.

> The spaces of New Babylon, as well as GAN-Physarum's Paris, have all the characteristics of a labyrinth, within which movement no longer submits to the constraints of given spatial or temporal organisation

Depending on the training input, this process results in the transfer of key features from one set of images onto another, and vice versa. In the case of the Parisian dérive, the domain of sourced images and target images refers to the slices of two actual input-images that belong in two different domains: the urban and the biological. This technique transfers the behavioural patterns of *Physarum polycephalum* onto the urban structure of Paris. The objective is to investigate how its biological intelligence can be applied on different scales to reinterpret existing infrastructures and building distributions of Paris itself.

While time-lapse photography, as described above, captures *Physarum polycephalum* at different developmental stages, Paris is analysed at different resolutions through remote sensing. A multiplicity of urban structures and urban morphological patterns can be detected while zooming in on the Centre Pompidou from a wide frame that includes the entire centre of Paris. By using descending orders of magnitude, the protocol captures frames of Paris at four different resolutions. The largest city scale is a 10 x 10 kilometre (6 x 6 mile) frame, including the entire circular Périphérique of Paris and centred on the site of the Centre Pompidou. While zooming in, further resolutions are registered: a 1 x 1 kilometre (0.62 mile) frame, showing the Centre Pompidou within its surrounding neighbourhood; a 100 x 100 metre (328 x 328 foot) frame, representing the structure of the Centre Pompidou with the adjacent streets and squares; and finally a 10 x 10 metre (32 x 32 foot) frame, focusing on the mechanical systems forming the external envelope of the celebrated Parisian architectural machine.

The Non-Human City

The machine-learning algorithm of GAN-Physarum is trained at each of these urban resolutions to a corresponding behavioural pattern of *Physarum polycephalum*. Over several generations, the algorithm learns how to reinterpret the *Physarum polycephalum*'s behaviours in relationship to Paris's morphological structures, and vice versa. This non-human cognitive process is underpinned by the GAN-Physarum's workflow developed by ecoLogicStudio and their team.

This workflow can be described in four main phases. First, the input images are prepared for training purposes. The dataset preparation is automated, slicing input images from both time-lapse and satellite source domains into equal tiles of 256 x 256 pixels in size. The second phase is the training of the GAN-Physarum based on these input datasets. At this stage, the model is sufficient for generating plausible slices in the target domain. The trained algorithm is then tested. During this phase, the GAN-Physarum projects an input image in the biological domain A to an image in the urban domain B, and vice versa. Several cached models from the training phase can be loaded at this stage, thus tracking the self-evolution of GAN-Physarum. In the fourth and final phase the output slices are automatically recombined into true-colour speculative satellite views.

Disorientation as a Design Practice

While at first sight the visions conjured by GAN-Physarum have the disorienting quality of the non-human mind that conceived them, they connect us with contemporary Paris at a more fundamental level. To paraphrase Constant, disorientation is favoured here as a design practice because it furthers adventure, play and creative change.

The spaces of New Babylon, as well as GAN-Physarum's Paris, have all the characteristics of a labyrinth, within which movement no longer submits to the constraints of given spatial or temporal organisation. In Constant's words, 'The labyrinth form of New Babylon's social space is the direct expression of social independence.'[7] ᴅ

Notes
1. Claudia Pasquero, 'Réseaux-Mondes', *Label Magazine*, 2022: https://label-magazine.com/en/art/articles/swiaty-sieci.
2. Mark Wigley, *Constant's New Babylon: The Hyper-Architecture of Desire*, Witte de With, Center For Contemporary Art/010 Publishers (Rotterdam), 1998, p 233.
3. Gilles Deleuze and Félix Guattari, *A Thousand Plateaus: Capitalism and Schizophrenia*, Bloomsbury (London), 1980.
4. Guy Debord, 'Theory of the Dérive', *Internationale Situationniste #2*, December 1958.
5. Claudia Pasquero and Marco Poletto, 'Culturalising the Microbiota: From High-Tech to Bio-Tech Architecture', in Mitra Kanaani (ed), *The Routledge Companion to Paradigms of Performativity in Design and Architecture*, Routledge (New York), 2021, pp 174–88.
6. Alec Radford, Luke Metz and Soumith Chintala, 'Unsupervised Representation Learning with Deep Convolutional Generative Adversarial Networks', International Conference on Learning Representations (ICLR), May 2016.
7. Constant Nieuwenhuys, 'New Babylon: Outline of a Culture', in *New Babylon*, tr Paul Hammond, Haags Gemeentemuseum (The Hague), 1974, pp 49–62.

Text © 2023 John Wiley & Sons Ltd. Images: pp 120–23 © NAARO; pp 124–6 © ecoLogicStudio

FROM ANOTHER PERSPECTIVE

A Word from *D* Editor
Neil Spiller

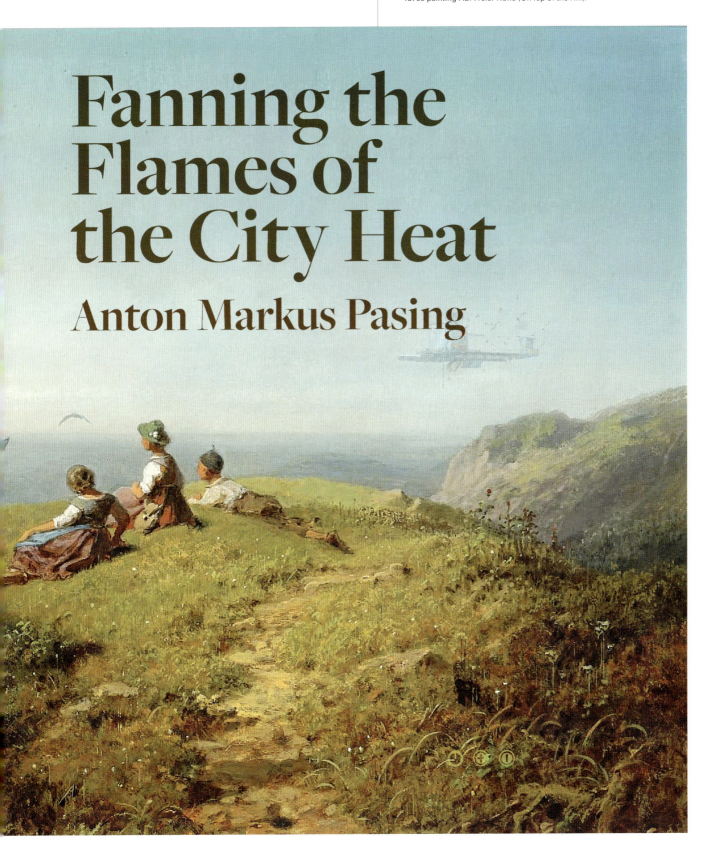

**Anton Markus Pasing,
Vaccine hunter 23,
2020**

Architecture is about time and timing. Here, Pasing creates the rather surreal image of one of his floating machines encountered by a group of figures in the German romanticist Carl Spitzweg's 1870s painting *Auf Freier Höhe (On Top of the Hill)*.

Fanning the Flames of the City Heat

Anton Markus Pasing

A city is for us a city only when it lets one feel multiplicity and discrepancy. High and low, density and emptiness, loud and quiet, heat and cold, tenderness and hardness, confusion and clarity held fast in possible structures.

— Coop Himmelblau, 1981[1]

'I think the contemporary city is a kind of purgatory, a self-promoting system that will eventually fall apart, not due to the architecture, but because the large populations of the city go against our nature,' says German designer Anton Markus Pasing, Professor of Architecture at the Peter Behrens School of Arts, University of Applied Sciences Düsseldorf. His perception is a variegated one: 'The city is a monster of information, emotion and density – an unpredictable beast. It is a place whose rate of growth does not adequately match its renewal. But it's also a place that fascinates me and shows me what I'm missing and what I don't need. It's good to visit a big city sometimes, but it's great to be able to leave it again.'

Anton Markus Pasing, The Recess, 2020

above: Plan perspective looking down on a portion of an imaginary city, portraying its mountainous landscape of caverns, grids and outcrops and provoking a slight feeling of vertigo in the viewer.

Anton Markus Pasing, City in a Box, part III: Paradox Memories (a reminiscence to 'Schroedingers cat'), 2019

Imagine an unknown city full of stories in a huge closed box. As long as the box is not opened, the city is quasi – in an 'intermediate state'; it is 50 per cent real and 50 per cent non-existent. The frenetic nature of the city, its multiscalar fractal interactions and its granular variations inspired this render. The juxtaposition of the familiar with the unfamiliar brought together in a hectic festival of colours, semiotics and textures is a trademark of the contemporary city.

Cities, Pasing believes, are full of nature, by which he means not just city parks or kerb-side weeds, or suburban gardens, but nature that incorporates the city's totality, including the cars, drains, building materials and airports. The city as he sees it, is an ubiquitous hybrid of the organic and the inorganic and not, as it is so often regarded, an uneasy reconciliation of these binary ontological opposites. This basic conceptual epistemology underpins all that he does, whether projecting that in drawings or models. 'Technology is pure nature, a highly specialised nature, which, however, is less complex than biological nature (first nature). It is an evolutionary side branch with absurd constellations and strategies which, however, significantly shape our culture.' According to Pasing, as machine beings we can no longer be separated. Man is present in machines through the persistence of our invention. What is inherent in machines is human reality. Therefore, in principle, any achievement made by machines is deeply human. We are inscribed in it and the modification of space it brings about is therefore always a cultural act.

Freedom of Expression

Pasing's initial architectural education was quite conservative and traditional. It was during his second degree at the Düsseldorf Art Academy, completed in 1991, that his work changed. It was there that he was given the confidence needed to work freely and seek intense forms of expression. It was in the late 1980s when he started to engage with the computer: 'My professor confronted me with the software called Swivel. A rudimentary program from today's perspective, but it fascinated me. However, my significant start in working with the computer was in 1998, when I got to know the Cinema 4D software. This has given my work decisive impetus. I was finally able to transfer my inner images into real graphics.' His dexterity with software gives his images considerable power and they are often exquisitely crafted, yet at the same time exhibiting the strange machinic hybridity of his worldview: 'For me everything is nature: technology, software, biology, everything. In it, the most diverse protagonists search for expression and functional purity, others for forgiveness and love. A vibrant hustle and bustle of picturesque shapes and colours. A possible extension of hybridity could be its destabilising capacity. Nothing is fixed. Time and impermanence will allow for a marriage of unknown potentials.'

It is this non-fixity and non-predictability of the future that also conditions Pasing's views on architectural education and the role of the academy. He believes that 'much architectural training is myopic', addressing itself too much to the now and not enough to the potential of the future and its massive, social, political and architectural ramifications: 'The most important thing is to educate students so that they are able to react flexibly and constructively to the changing requirements and questions of the time, that they fill their hearts with passion for architecture, that they develop a high level of resilience to stupidity and live out their emotions mercilessly.'

When it comes to Pasing's work, the tight form/function relationship is considered one-dimensional, lacking in what he calls the 'meta-level'. This absent meta-level is problematic in many architecture schools globally, because of the frequent pedagogic reliance on modernist ideas of a hundred or so years ago and their now mostly outdated technologies. The use of narrative is important to him; without narrative, architecture work is nothing. The handing-down of tired dogmas and doctrines from one generation of architects to their students inhibits the creative metabolic rate he so often espouses. Pasing is in favour of producing much more autonomous students and, vicariously, architectural education and creativity: 'I would also prefer a teaching model in which students train each other and only involve professors as advisors on demand. This would increase independence enormously.'

Utopian or Dystopian

In line with the theme of this ⌀, Pasing's work can seem both utopian or dystopian depending on the viewer's architectural proclivities. However, it is always graphically and compositionally audacious and thought-provoking: 'I never intend how any of my work should be read. The image is always its own meta-language that eludes the codes of language. The interpretation can not only be dystopian or utopian, but also evoke any other connotation that arises between the viewer and the image.' For Pasing as an architect, there is an ever-present creative imperative that drives him on, not particularly cognisant of whether he pleases others but enjoying the feeling when people like his output; 'With my work, I pursue no other goals than to share my inner images and speculations, to ask questions. If my work appears dystopian to a viewer, this is the purely subjective interpretation of the viewer. If my work inspires anyone or pleases them, that is wonderfully healing for me. If not, I still have to keep going. The passion for the story dies last.'

Operating in this way, as Pasing does, is a constant quest to reconcile the differing and often both positive and negative emotions arising from his shifting perceptions of the world – its joys and its predicaments. This means that his working methodology changes over time and never stays constant: 'The parameters of my working method vary with my perception, because I always refer to my own individual conception of the world. I'm not looking for truth or a higher purpose for society. I deal with things that touch me, both positively and negatively.'

Anton Markus Pasing,
Rotor Baron (Red Baron) 'R-AON',
2014

Pasing sometimes collects *objets trouvés* from the discarded detritus of the city and then assembles them to create anthropomorphic architectural forms that illustrate his ideas of the spectrum of technologies caricatured in the machinic ecologies of the contemporary urban environment.

But Pasing's oeuvre consists of more than two-dimensional computer plots and renders. He takes pleasure in modelling from found objects and combining his discoveries in what might be described as three-dimensional Surrealist exquisite corpses. In contrast to the hands-off manipulation of virtual forms within the digital screen, the haptic and visceral is deeply important to Pasing and his working methods: 'There are times and moments when I am no longer able to endure the stillness and the two-dimensionality of the computer screen. Every day, 12 hours, and at the end you feel like you haven't done anything. Then it is a must for me to create real, physical objects and pay homage to three-dimensionality. Also, in my experience, other things come about when you work with your hands. The signal change in the brain seems to be different. It's more intuitive. I don't plan to build, I just start. I searched for stones, roots and similar things in the forest for a very long time in order to then turn them into new hybrid protagonists of my stories.[2] Model-making is the artistic act that gives me the most satisfaction, both artistically and physically.'

Anton Markus Pasing,
TLJ-Alpha I: The Last Journey Machine (good luck said the frog),
2019

It has often been speculated that the modern city has much in common with the architectures of electronic circuit boards. Here, this phenomenon is presented as a vision of architectural indeterminacy.

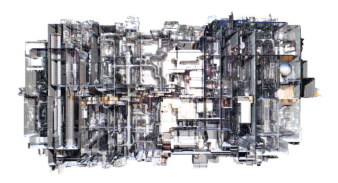

So What of Architecture?

For an architect whose work is extremely speculative and questions the nature of the future city, the limits of our bodies and our shifting relationships with evolving technology, Pasing is strangely romantic in the way he relishes the millennia-old basic ontology of architecture: 'I'm not a prophet, but I sincerely believe that the core principles will not change: homeland, a home, a roof to protect you, a territory to live in peace, a nest to keep you warm, and a place you share only with loved ones, sharing places, and places that inspire you. Despite all the technology, I hope this will never change. And if it does, I don't want to be a part of it.'

But he also understands that change is here to stay. This exploration of change is an intensive part of his architectural explorations and he is optimistic about aspects of it: 'The relationships between mobility and immobility will also change, presumably becoming more unstable. I also think perception will increasingly change from a spatial to a visual experience, which can already be observed in the culture of today's youth. I think there will be exciting times.'

So, for Pasing, as for any good architect, navigating our complex world is a field of contradictions – emotionally, technologically, culturally and socially: 'Two hearts beat in my chest; one still wants to tell stories, the other just wants to "be". I long for autonomy in my work, which I am just beginning to do and I realise it's a tightrope walk. I don't want to explain anything, I don't want to justify myself. I ask more questions than I have answers. In the end, my goal is to no longer feel my difference to my body.'

This rather existential series of thoughts defines the wonderful world of Anton Markus Pasing and his long, beautiful – and sometimes disturbing – journey in creating his own architectural odyssey and lexicon. ⌂

This article is based on an email interview and correspondence with Anton Markus Pasing during March 2022.

Notes
1. Coop Himmelblau, *Die Faszination Der Stadt/The Power of the City*, Verlag der G Buchner Buchhandlung (Darmstadt), 1988, p 22.
2. Anton Markus Pasing, *Eutopia 2: Non-Linear Multiple Hybrid Solutions*, Revolver Publishing (Berlin), 2014.

Anton Markus Pasing,
I just can't stand the Draft,
2022

The technologies of the city coalesce into a continuous skein of metallic and architecturally penetrating machinic mycelium, connecting everything to everything else.

Text © 2023 John Wiley & Sons Ltd. Images: p 128(t) © Robbie Munn; pp 128–9(b), 130–33 © Anton Markus Pasing / Remote-controlled studio

URBAN DYSTOPIAS

Tridib Banerjee is Professor Emeritus of Public Policy at the University of Southern California (USC), where he previously held the James Irvine Chair in Urban and Regional Planning. He is co-author of *Beyond the Neighborhood Unit* (Springer, 1984) and *Urban Design Downtown* (University of California Press, 1998), and co-edited *City Sense and City Design: Writings and Projects of Kevin Lynch* (MIT Press, 1990), *The Companion to Urban Design* and *The New Companion to Urban Design* (Routledge, 2011 and 2019). He also edited the four-volume set *Urban Design: Critical Concepts in Urban Studies* (Routledge, 2014). His most recent publication is *In the Images of Development: City Design in the Global South* (MIT Press, 2021).

Daniele Belleri is a design editor and a partner at CRA-Carlo Ratti Associati, where he is in charge of all editorial and curatorial projects. He was executive curator at the 2019 Bi-City Biennale of Urbanism and Architecture (UABB) in Shenzhen, and ran CRA's Urban Study for Manifesta 14 Prishtina. He previously co-founded a London-based strategic design agency, was a researcher and taught at the Strelka Institute for Media, Architecture and Design in Moscow, and worked as an independent journalist contributing to international media including Reuters, the *Corriere della Sera*, *Wired* and *Volume*.

Stephen Glackin is Senior Research Fellow at the Centre for Urban Transitions, Swinburne University of Technology. He is currently investigating the factors required for sustainable urban transformation. These include urban planning, statutory regimes, community engagement, financial feasibility analysis, design (urban and built form), the data/software required by stakeholders to optimise the above, and the governance models for cities. Associated research includes geospatial analysis of urban environments, collating large datasets across jurisdictional (state, municipal and infrastructural governance) boundaries, and developing decision support systems for planners and urban stakeholders.

Justyna Karakiewicz is Professor of Architecture and Urban Design in the Faculty of Architecture, Building and Planning at the University of Melbourne. She previously taught at the Architectural Association (AA) in London, Bartlett School of Architecture, University College London (UCL), University of Hong Kong and many other institutions. She is co-author of *The Making of Hong Kong* (Routledge, 2010), *Promoting Sustainable Living: Sustainability as an Object of Desire* (Routledge, 2015) and *Urban Galapagos* (Springer, 2018), and has published more than 70 papers and book chapters. She has won numerous international competitions and has been awarded many prizes for her drawings. Her work has been exhibited around the world including at the Venice Architecture Biennale.

Nano Langenheim is a lecturer in Landscape Architecture and Urban Design at the University of Melbourne. Her research focus is the transdisciplinary modelling of streetscapes, and the evolution of algorithmic botany or tree structural modelling, from L-systems through to advanced recursive branching, procedural and space colonisation algorithms. She trained as an arborist before undertaking her PhD in urban forest design at Monash University Faculty of Art, Design and Architecture (MADA) in Australia, extensively studying the history of trees in cities, examining the evolution and shifts in design decision drivers for street networks, and particularly street trees, from the traditionally visual and functional to the environmental imperatives of today.

Mehrnoush Latifi is a lecturer, researcher and currently the course director of the Bachelor of Design (Architecture) at Swinburne University of Technology in Melbourne. She was previously Industry Fellow for the Master of Design Innovation and Technology (MDIT) programme at the city's RMIT University. She completed her PhD at RMIT's Spatial Information Architecture Laboratory (SIAL) in 2018. She leads the Smart Skins for Smarter Cities transdisciplinary research team as part of the Future Urban Infrastructure programme at Swinburne's Smart Cities Research Institute (SCRI). Her creative practice, research and teaching span the fields of architecture, virtual and augmented reality, thermal comfort, microclimate design and digital fabrication. Her work has been exhibited as part of national and international exhibitions including 'Dynamics of Air' (RMIT Gallery, 2018), and at the Craft ACT: Craft + Design Centre (Canberra, 2015 and 2016).

Andong Lu received his BArch from Tsinghua University in Beijing, and his MPhil and PhD from the University of Cambridge, where he was a Fellow of Wolfson College and Isaac Newton Trust Fellow. He is currently Lead Professor in Urban Design and Vice-Dean of the School of Architecture and Urban Planning at Nanjing University. He is the China representative of the International Union of Architects (UIA) Work Programme on Public Space, and a board member of the Committee of Urban Design, Committee of Architectural Critics and Committee of Architectural Media of the Architectural Society of China. He served as chief curator of the Chinese Pavilion at the London Design Biennale (2018), chief curator of the 9th Shenzhen Bi-city Biennale of Urbanism\Architecture (2022), and as masterplanner of the UNESCO City of Literature, Nanjing.

Dan Nyandega is a lecturer in Landscape Architecture and Urbanism at Queensland University of Technology (QUT) in Brisbane, Australia. He has a PhD in architecture (water-sensitive design) from Monash University, and a MArch from KU Leuven in Belgium. His PhD was under a multidisciplinary platform Cooperative Research Centre for Water Sensitive Cities (CRCWSC) and MADA urban lab at Monash. He has taught architecture at Monash, and landscape architecture at RMIT University. His design-led research explores the intersection of coastal cities infrastructures, landscapes, architecture and rising water levels.

Jordi Oliveras is Professor at Universitat Politècnica de Catalunya in Barcelona, where he teaches Contemporary

CONTRIBUTORS

Architecture Issues in Master's studies. He is a specialist in the history of urbanism, and a scholar in modern and contemporary architectural history, museums and mass housing. He is the author of *New Populations of the Enlightenment* (Arquia, 1998).

Kas Oosterhuis is an innovator, writer, educator and a practising designer. He leads the innovation studio ONL [Oosterhuis_Lénárd], which he runs with his partner in life and business, visual artist Ilona Lénárd. The studio has realised bespoke buildings including the Saltwater Pavilion (Neeltje Jans, the Netherlands 1997), A20 Cockpit commercial building (Rotterdam, 2019), Bálna Budapest cultural centre (Budapest, 2013) and LIWA tower (Abu Dhabi, 2014). He was professor at Delft University of Technology (TU Delft) from 2000 to 2016, and at Qatar University from 2017 to 2019. He is the author of *Towards a New Kind of Building* (NAi Publishers, 2010), and is currently writing a new book titled *Interacting Components: A Personal Odyssey*.

Claudia Pasquero is an architect, curator, author and educator whose work and research operate at the intersection of biology, computation and design. She is co-founder, with Marco Poletto, of the architectural practice ecoLogicStudio in London, Landscape Architecture Professor at Innsbruck University and Associated Professor at the Bartlett, UCL. In 2017 she was Head Curator of the Tallinn Architectural Biennale, and a nominee in the WIRED smart list the same year. She is co-author, with Poletto, of *Systemic Architecture: Operating Manual for the Self-Organizing City* (Routledge, 2012) and the forthcoming *DeepGreen: Bio-design in the Age of Artificial Intelligence*. Her work has been exhibited internationally. ecoLogicStudio has successfully completed a number of photosynthetic architectures, such as PhotosSynthEtica (Helsinki, 2020) and AirBubble Playground (Warsaw, 2021).

Marco Poletto is an architect, educator and innovator based in London. He is co-founder (with Claudia Pasquero) and Director of ecoLogicStudio, and the design innovation venture PhotoSynthEtica, focused on developing architectural solutions to fight climate change. He holds a PhD from RMIT University. His thesis on the 'Urbansphere' argues that the increased spatial integration of non-human systems within architecture is crucial to evolve higher forms of urban ecological intelligence. He has been a Unit Master at the AA, visiting critic at Cornell University in Ithaca, New York, and Research Cluster leader at the Bartlett, UCL. He currently lectures at the University of Innsbruck and the Institute for Advanced Architecture of Catalonia (IAAC) in Barcelona. His work has been exhibited internationally.

Carlo Ratti is an architect and engineer by training. He teaches at the Massachusetts Institute of Technology (MIT) in Cambridge, where he directs the Senseable City Lab. He is also a founding partner of design and innovation office CRA-Carlo Ratti Associati, based in Turin, with branches in New York City and London. His work contributed to advancing the debate on the impact of new technologies on urban life. His projects have been exhibited in venues worldwide, including at the Venice Architecture Biennale and Museum of Modern Art (MoMA) in New York. He is currently serving as co-chair of the World Economic Forum's Global Future Council on Cities and Urbanization.

Neil Spiller is Editor of *D*, and was previously Hawksmoor Chair of Architecture and Landscape and Deputy Pro Vice Chancellor at the University of Greenwich in London. Prior to this he was Vice Dean at the Bartlett School of Architecture, UCL. He has made an international reputation as an architect, designer, artist, teacher, writer and polemicist. He is the founding director of the Advanced Virtual and Technological Architecture Research (AVATAR) group, which continues to push the boundaries of architectural design and discourse in the face of the impact of 21st-century technologies. Its current preoccupations include augmented and mixed realities and other metamorphic technologies.

Dr Ian Woodcock is Senior Lecturer in Urbanism at the Sydney School of Architecture, Design and Planning, the University of Sydney, and Adjunct Associate Professor in the Centre for Design Innovation, School of Design and Architecture, Swinburne University of Technology. He has published widely on urban transformation and place identity, often drawing insights from speculative multi-scale design research for sustainable mobility environments.

Tianyi Yang is an award-winning Australian architect, researcher and lecturer with experience in cutting-edge academic research at the Swinburne University of Technology and the University of Melbourne. Her focus is on designing a sustainable and liveable urban future using data and emerging technologies. She is completing her doctoral studies on informing healthcare facility design under the NOVELL Redesign project. She has been involved in numerous significant design projects, working with practices in China, Europe and Australia. Her design work has been exhibited worldwide, including at WantedDesign in New York and OCAT Shanghai.

Kongjian Yu received his Doctor of Design from Harvard Graduate School of Design (GSD) in Cambridge, Massachusetts. He is a Professor and Founding Dean of the Peking University College of Architecture and Landscape, and founder and principal designer of landscape architects Turenscape. Several of his core ideas have been adopted for nationwide implementation by the Chinese government and had global reach. His projects have won international design awards, including 14 American Society of Landscape Architects (ASLA) Excellence and Honor awards, and five World Architecture Festival (WAF) Best Landscape Architecture of the Year awards. He is a member of the American Academy of Arts and Sciences, and received the International Federation of Landscape Architects' Sir Geoffrey Jellicoe Award in 2020.

What is *Architectural Design*?

Founded in 1930, *Architectural Design* (△) is an influential and prestigious publication. It combines the currency and topicality of a newsstand journal with the rigour and production qualities of a book. With an almost unrivalled reputation worldwide, it is consistently at the forefront of cultural thought and design.

Issues of △ are edited either by the journal Editor, Neil Spiller, or by an invited Guest-Editor. Renowned for being at the leading edge of design and new technologies, △ also covers themes as diverse as architectural history, the environment, interior design, landscape architecture and urban design.

Provocative and pioneering, △ inspires theoretical, creative and technological advances. It questions the outcome of technical innovations as well as the far-reaching social, cultural and environmental challenges that present themselves today.

For further information on △, subscriptions and purchasing single issues see:

https://onlinelibrary.wiley.com/journal/15542769

Volume 92 No 1
ISBN 978 1119 743255

Volume 92 No 2
ISBN 978 1119 748793

Volume 92 No 3
ISBN 978 1119 748847

Volume 92 No 4
ISBN 978 1119 787778

Volume 92 No 5
ISBN 978 1119 833932

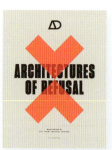

Volume 92 No 6
ISBN 978 1119 833963

Individual backlist issues of △ are available as books for purchase starting at £29.99 / US$45.00

wiley.com

How to Subscribe
With 6 issues a year, you can subscribe to △ either print or online.

https://onlinelibrary.wiley.com/journal/15542769

Institutional subscription
£357 / US$666
online only

£373 / US$695
print only

£401 / US$748
print and online

Personal-rate subscription
£151 / US$236
print only

Student-rate subscription
£97 / US$151
print only

Individual issue:
£9.99 / US$13.99

To subscribe to print or online
E: cs-journals@wiley.com
W: https://onlinelibrary.wiley.com/journal/15542769

Americas
E: cs-journals@wiley.com
T: +1 877 762 2974

Europe, Middle East and Africa
E: cs-journals@wiley.com
T: +44 (0)18 6577 8315

Asia Pacific
E: cs-journals@wiley.com
T: +65 6511 8000

Japan (for Japanese-speaking support)
E: cs-japan@wiley.com
T: +65 6511 8010

Visit our Online Customer Help
available in 7 languages at www.wileycustomerhelp.com/ask